The Bumper Book of Health & Care Workforce Planning

Contents

Foreword

Workforce Transformation is at one level a strange term, as it implies the need for a radical re-think of what is essentially the NHS' greatest asset. But it is a term, like it or not, which has got traction over recent years, as pressures upon health and care services escalate and diversify; more people living longer, but not necessarily living well; advancing technologies forcing change to service models and ways of working; and what better example of a 'burning platform' than the recent pandemic, pushing the NHS and our workforce to the very limit in a totally unprecedented way. But regardless of what we call it, redesign of care models triggered by our current reality, goes hand in glove with redesign of the workforce. And that's where this book comes in...

Workforce planning, modelling and redesign can be difficult; it really is a case of having to choose your attitude - not least because the job is large, often complex and the time available is limited. We need an army of people with wide-ranging and quite different skills, from data analytics to large scale change, from educationalists to innovators and everything in between - oh and time, consistent focus and endless energy...

At Health Education England, we have focused on providing the tools and techniques to do just that, including the HEE Star diagnostic tool and the clinically-led CLEAR workforce redesign education programme. Alongside these, this book provides a pragmatic approach to workforce redesign for leaders, managers and clinicians alike, and includes the broader considerations about workforce planning and the infrastructure required to drive continuous improvement of workforce in health and care systems.

Having worked alongside Colin, Fiona and Amina for the last 8 years, both on the development of the WRaPT workforce model and in the early days of workforce collaboratives in Greater Manchester, I know that this book is based on real world experience. I hope that the approaches set out here, will give you the appetite, the confidence, the attitude to approach workforce planning and redesign with structure and gusto. Good luck!

Kirstie Baxter

Head of Workforce Transformation

Health Education England

Introduction

In 1993, Meatloaf was in the charts with, "I'd do anything for love". Jurassic Park was in the cinema. A Freddo cost 10p. It was also the year that I started a job with a retailer called Martin Retail Group, that turned out to involve a heady mix of workforce planning and training.

By 2000, Health Trust Turnaround had started, and so I applied these same approaches to health and care organisations to help them balance budgets. Twenty years on and I'm still in health & care, although now it's all about workforce planning to meet increasing demand with fewer of the traditional staff available. I'm sure money will be important again at some point though...

Seven years ago, I was lucky enough to be involved in developing the Workforce Repository and Planning Tool (WRaPT) with Kirstie Baxter of Health Education England and Craig Barratt of Lancashire Care Foundation Trust. This is where I teamed up with Fiona Lord and Amina Jina, and we now spend our days training people in the many and varied aspects of workforce planning. And our nights fighting crime, but that's a tale for another book.

Of course, when I started in health back in the last millennia, many managers were used to workforce planning, but years of chasing waiting lists and a lack of investment in their development has seen this skillset degrade just when it is needed the most. New Integrated Care Systems and Partnerships and a rise in the importance of Primary Care Networks has created a whole new set of managers for whom workforce planning is an absolutely vital skill.

This book aims to help develop the skills of managers by providing a guide and associated wisdom from nearly thirty years of workforce planning. It includes approaches to workforce redesign, developing workforce plans, organisational and team workforce planning and building workforce hubs. It truly is a Bumper Book of Health & Care Workforce Planning.

It is designed for any manager in health or care. It's for Primary Care Network and Practice Managers, for Community and Social Care Team Leaders, for Operations Directors, Divisional Managers, Directorate Managers and Ward Managers. It's for HR teams, Primary Care training hubs and ICS and ICP Workforce Leads. Basically, it's for anyone who runs a team or needs to plan health and care workforce at system, organisation or team level.

Colin Lewry

SECTION ONE

AN INTRODUCTION TO WORKFORCE PLANNING

There are more than three million people working in the NHS and Social Care across the UK, and that doesn't include the army of volunteers and carers that work tirelessly to deliver care.

This health and care workforce is an amazing group of people, but it is one that any credible commentator reports is facing insufficient supply in the face of rising demand, and it is one that needs to transform.

Not only does it need to transform, but it has a massive opportunity to improve performance through transformation. Population Health Data, new digital tools, new roles, remote healthcare, new models and pathways, Primary Care transformation, social resilience, new treatments and approaches can all be grasped to improve health, patient experience and staff satisfaction.

One of the approaches available to drive transformation and reduce the gap between capacity and demand is Workforce Planning. This is the approach used to anticipate staffing needs and to build a workforce that has the people with the right knowledge, experience and skills in the right place at the right time. It is a solution to many of the long list of challenges and opportunities of the current workforce situation.

It is also a handy and variable set of skills and approaches to create the perfect balance between demand and workforce supply whether in the smallest team, the largest health and care system or nationally. In a small team, it could consider day to day requirements in the face of shifting demand. In an Integrated Care System (ICS) it could consist of multiple team and pathway workforce plans and models, which will be combined and co-ordinated to ensure that there is a coherent workforce strategy and plan for the entire system.

I keep using the term "workforce", because I've lost all my humanity and now sound like Data from Star Trek. And that's the sort of cutting-edge popular culture reference you are going to get from me throughout this book. Other people might say "Human Resources" or "Labor" if you are in the United States. Of course, we are really talking about what humans would call "people", individuals and not some amorphous group. People with their own skills, attitudes, needs, feelings, biases and abilities which will be different to everyone else.

Of course, this means treating the subject with respect first and foremost. But it should also be considered in the plan because treating people like people means having the right roles, career structures and incentives that help people enjoy their role and career. It also means not assuming anything until you have involved them. I've known people engage in workshops and come up with the most forward-thinking new model, only for it to fall apart completely during implementation when it's suggested they sit in a room with someone who eats sprouts from a flask for lunch.

Throughout this book I will talk about the workforce, but I mean people. I will also talk about patients or 'service-users'. In all cases, I try to never lose sight of the fact that they are all real people.

Workforce planning is also never finished and is always changing. I will talk later about the different types of workforce planning, from day to day operational to long-term strategic planning. No matter where you are on that scale, workforce planning is only working completely if the needs of service-users are being met by the right people, in the right place, with the right skills and attitudes at the right time, every time. It'll never be perfect, and is never over.

It also isn't done on its own. For any system to work it needs the right people, but also the right facilities, right processes, right organisational structures and the right equipment and technology. Workforce planning cannot be done completely without these other elements.

Often, when you are asked to do workforce planning, you have to undertake a complete system redesign. It's just that workforce is the driver, the most common problem or just the angle.

Other times the need for cost reduction or better outcomes can be the driver for system redesign, which will then include workforce planning.

Workforce planning is therefore lots of things. It is about meeting demand with the right workforce, about working with real people, it is never ending and is interconnected with wider elements. And it is absolutely, 100% necessary at all times, and never more so than now in Health & Social Care.

Chapter 1.1

What is Workforce Planning?

Let's talk through what workforce planning is and what it consists of, to allow us to have a shared view of what we mean when we say, "workforce planning". Whilst this might seem basic stuff, it is a fundamental step in actually getting workforce planning done.

Health Education England (HEE) define Workforce Planning, as:

"to support the delivery of excellent healthcare and health improvement to the patients and public of England by ensuring that the workforce of today and tomorrow has the right numbers, skills, values and behaviours, at the right time and in the right place"

This is a very wide definition, because it includes everything from day-to-day discussions about whether we need to call someone else in because Geoff hasn't turned up again, to funding places for a thousand nurses nationally, and everything in between. And there is a hell of a lot in between.

Workforce Planning is therefore done from short operational timescales to long term strategic horizons:

Day to Day

In the shortest term, we have to take account of those day-to-day small changes, like the ever-problematic Geoff and whether we need to authorise overtime or bring in temporary staffing for short-term issues. Slightly longer term, we have the handling of natural workforce evolution: A GP leaves, a secretary retires, someone wants more hours or demand drops unexpectedly.

This requires ongoing evolution of staffing to continue to match demand with a quality staffing response.

The questions you ask are: What gaps exist today in my staffing? Does who I have in meet the needs/ acuity of the service-users? Do I need to change anything right now?

The core skills you need are team management and leadership skills, because what is happening is so short-term and in the moment.

Short-Term

On a weekly, monthly or up to annual basis you will need to match workforce to demand through rotas, and manage planned absence. You'll also need to deal with long-term absence where it appears, deciding whether to replace staff that will be off work for an extended period. You also need to consider the development of the team, building skills to match the changing needs of service-users.

The questions you ask are: What is my plan and rota? What can I do with the budget of this person who is leaving? How does my team need to develop?

The skills you need include rostering, managing absence, coaching and mentoring.

Annual

Perhaps more embedded in the psyche of acute trusts about ten years ago, the annual planning cycle takes us into the mid-term stuff. NHS Improvement/England (NHSI/E) in its Monitor days produced an excellent approach called Service Line Management (SLM), which included a description of an annual (and strategic process) and is still available on t'Internet.

This included a great approach to annual planning that I still use today. Annual planning provides a chance to look at demand projections, budget, your team, the strategy, changes in practice and technology etc, to adjust your staffing model for the following year. Often linked to the appraisal and other processes, an annual process allows you to look at training, recruitment and tactical changes to your team.

The question you ask at this level is: What team is needed in the next year to meet our strategy?

The skills you need include managing activity and team to budget, workforce redesign and developing workforce plans.

Long-Term

You also need to look at long-term planning. These are changes that will take two to five years, looking at the strategic picture years out and looking at how you can build the right team to meet perhaps a very different demand profile. This is often more transformation than evolution, and because of the challenge we face in health and social care there are few services that don't need to do this now.

Strategic

Finally, there is a strategic picture: Strategic Workforce Planning. This is the Executive, System, Regional or National stuff that anticipates the future and prepares anything beyond five years.

The questions you are asking here are the most strategic: What team is needed to meet the long term strategy? How do I generate a staff pipeline? How do I redesign to be relevant in the future?

Skills required are workforce redesign, developing workforce plans and building of collaboratives.

So, workforce planning operates across multiple timeframes, each of which require different skills. From day-to-day management, through rostering, mentoring, coaching, and managing costs to redesign, planning and the development of collaboratives.

Chapter 1.2

Why Learn About Workforce Planning?

The Health and Social Care sector really needs to get on with some serious workforce planning. Without it, we are going to continue to struggle to deliver the outcomes people deserve, burn out the hard-working people that we have and fail to deliver an efficient, effective service.

With it, we can take advantage of the need to transform to build patient and staff-focused services that deliver vastly improved outcomes through efficient processes, enhanced digital offers, new multi-disciplinary teams, new and improved roles and more appropriate therapies. That's why we need to learn about workforce planning.

But what, when we come down to brass tacks, is in it for you? Well, that depends on who you are and where you work in:

Regional and System Workforce Teams

You may have been given responsibility for "workforce", either totally across your region or system, or for a workstream.

And I can tell you from working with lots of people that get this "development opportunity", that it can be an utter nightmare. You have to go to meetings for ten hours a day, to be asked, "Where is workforce up to?", and to be blamed for there not being a workforce plan, or not enough workforce to do something. It is not great.

For these fun and games to end, you need a prioritised plan based on what is important, not necessarily what everyone else wants you to do. You also need a basis to be able to point out that workforce isn't just your responsibility, so why doesn't everyone work together to transform all aspects of delivery rather than just asking for workforce transformation?

And while you are at it, wouldn't it be great to have a standard approach you can use, a development programme for teams to be able to do this themselves, and a tool they can all record everything in? Of course it would.

Front-Line and Management Teams

You have responsibility for delivering great care for your service-users with a great team, working within a budget. Hopefully you don't do this on your own, and have support from clinical managers of various flavours (for example, Clinical Director orNurse Director.

Ask yourself these questions: Do you need to be able to plan your workforce every year in response to an annual planning process? Do you not have exactly the team you need at the moment but want to build one? Do you struggle to meet demand?

Well, workforce planning is the approach to use to start solving these problems. It's also the approach to use to transform your workforce with the help of your people, and to develop a plan to maintain a great team over years by looking into the future and planning ahead. And, if you have difficulty in managing to a budget, this is also the approach to either improve efficiency, or to be able to actually prove to finance that the budget is wrong. That last bit might not make a difference, but you'll feel better...

Practice and Network Managers

Suddenly, people are realising something you've known for years: Primary Care is the answer. New roles are being planned, new technology like Population Health Management is appearing. Social prescribing, community resilience, prevention, case management and home monitoring through Alexa are being talked about (I'm not selling anything, other systems are also available - you can shout into a can with a really tight piece of string attached if you like).

You need a new workforce model and a plan to implement it, while working in a somewhat time-poor environment. Workforce planning is the answer, and this standard approach works well if applied to any other workforce planning tools that the Primary Care Training Hub chooses.

Community and Social Care Team Leaders

It's all about community these days, right? Suddenly we all need locality teams that respond to the needs of Primary Care. Or we need to operate open-access services. Or we need to pick up work that used to be done in acute sites.

Workforce planning is the answer to working out how on earth this is going to be done, and what roles we can use to meet demand, especially in working out what teams are big enough to work locally, and what needs to be a bit more central.

Acute Trust Service Managers

Back in the days before minute-by-minute waiting list management, you used to do strategic workforce planning as part of your job, but these days it is all about getting overwhelming demand through your services with the people you have available. At the same time, Cost Improvement Plans (CIPs) are still mentioned annually, although they tend to have been replaced with regular updates on how much you've missed your budget by.

Workforce planning and redesign is a great way to get on the front foot and engage your team in developing an evidenced-based plan to get better outcomes for staff and service-users. And prove to finance that these are the people that you need.

Organisation Executives

Your people are your single biggest asset, and they are getting increasingly scarce. Developing your front-line teams to plan their workforce requirements and develop their transformation ideas is a great way to ensure that people are more valued – and they know their services better than anyone. Also, developing an evidenced-based view on who you need to manage the ever-growing demand, rather than relying purely on financial projections would be great, right?

Through effective workforce planning, you can have a happier workforce, better outcomes for service-users, and a more efficient operation, and have a clear plan to show to everyone else.

So, workforce planning has pretty significant advantages for most roles in health and social care. This book is designed for managers, which can include clinicians - but clinicians and care deliverers should also learn this skillset and get involved. You can use this approach, or specifically designed approaches for clinicians, like CLEAR.

The trouble is, that it isn't easy, as we'll discuss in the next chapter…

Chapter 1.3

Why Workforce Planning is Impossible

So that all sounds great so far. The trouble is, it is (almost) impossible to do it properly and efficiently. That's no excuse not to try, because it is a battle worth fighting, but just don't expect it to be easy. Teams are surviving every day with insufficient staff to deliver demand, people can't find enough staff to fill vacancies and central teams can't get new roles adopted. Not because people forgot how to do workforce planning, but because something has got in the way.

It has got to the point that in the last year or so, large-scale workforce transformation has become, to some extent, impossible in health and care in England. I believe it is almost impossible because there are so many barriers that not enough people have the position, strength, skill and sheer bloody-mindedness to make it happen.

I want to set out these barriers, because I see people working incredibly hard to make workforce transformation a reality and I want to be able to at least tell them I understand their pain. Perhaps also by understanding these barriers together we can acknowledge the difficulties as a group of professionals and reflect them in our discussions with those that can help. And we might be able to make the job a little bit easier while we are waiting for the structural changes that we need, and that will come. At some point. Eventually.

In summary, we have a problem. The sheer scale of the challenge is very large, and bold change is required to meet it. Because of this scale, transformation activities are being driven from multiple viewpoints by multiple agencies and are not adequately co-ordinated. Local co-ordination is practically impossible because there are complex organisational boundaries and no clarity on who makes the hard decisions. There is also little co-ordination within functions of the system or the same organisation – with finance having to provide information on workforce numbers that don't align with bottom-up planning done by front-line teams. On top of all this, there is so much else going on that there aren't enough people with enough skills in redesign or enough time to do it.

Overall, structural change is needed to address this: Clear system responsibility with a mandate to undertake bold change, supported by aligned national and regional support. A significant investment in resources to deliver a large-scale transformation programme will only then be able to address the enormous opportunity to transform that the health and care sector faces. More detailed issues include:

The Sheer Scale of the Challenge

First, the whole transformation challenge is enormous. The effort involved in bringing together health and social care, developing neighbourhood teams and integrated primary care, new pathways taking account of remote working opportunities and integrating new and expanding technology like Artificial Intelligence (AI) or Robotic Process Automation (RPA) is enormous. As I have said, this brings great opportunity as well, but the challenge is the same: It seems an impossible task already because it is so big and by the time we've got round it once, we'll be starting again.

Solution: Desmond Tutu once asked – "How do you eat an elephant?" I understand that this was a rhetorical question and not a request for

information on a practical problem, because he also provided the answer, "a bit at a time".

There is plenty to go around, so we've got to prioritise, build capacity to do the job, provide the time to do it, plan and get on with it.

The Need for Bold Change

Of course, the above is a problem already, but the need and the opportunity for the health and care sector is for bold change. This will take a lot of time to achieve, because things are going to change for real people doing real jobs. But it is also going to result in significant organisational issues with staff and funding flowing between providers. The bottom line is that bold change is, well, impossible as a result.

Workforce Transformation is Transformation

One of the reasons why the scale of workforce transformation needed is so big, is that it isn't just about workforce redesign: Transformation also needs us to look at process, organisation structure, technology, equipment and facilities.

We're in a strange situation at the moment where those responsible for workforce transformation are being asked: "Where are your workforce transformation plans?" The reality is that workforce transformation should be done as part of an overall transformation to take account of all of the above. We regularly find ourselves being asked to do workforce redesign but discover that there is not even an Information Governance framework in place, let alone a transformed care model either developed or being developed. As a result, workforce transformation needs to do the whole project. Which is a bit rough, but can be done, although it tends to end up blowing the budget somewhat, and even with adequate funding we end up clashing with other groups that are responsible for transformation in general.

Solution: Systems and organisations should stop asking for workforce transformation plans and should instead define the priorities for redesign across the system and pull together a combined team of transformation experts (which should include workforce transformation), working under a single governance process.

Excellent. So, we just need to do a complete transformation not just a workforce transformation. That's a bigger job, but possible. Right?

Complex Overlapping Boundaries

It's possible, yes, but there are some more barriers in the way. The next one is that undertaking that complete transformation is made very difficult by overlapping complex organisational boundaries.

Healthcare is a fractured mix of providers, commissioners and other bodies. It sometimes feels that everyone is in charge. Is the ICS or Sustainability and Transformation Programme (STP) in charge? Possibly, but that isn't even a statutory organisation at the time of writing, so relies on agreement somewhat. Maybe we'll find it's a secondary care led situation? But GPs are independent, and we all know that there is a huge opportunity to transform how care is delivered with Primary Care at the heart, so shouldn't change be led there? And once we add in social care, well they work under a completely different set of legal rules to healthcare. And while we're at it, what is the regional role? What about Cancer Networks, and other such clinical groups? And then we have different central roles within HEE and within NHSI/E. Blimey.

Solution: Getting anything done at the moment requires long-term co-operation and, often, putting aside local and national rules. And that co-operation, almost impossible though it is to build, needs to be maintained. The only real solution comes from those higher up the chain – realistically at national level, sorting out who is actually responsible for getting this done.

Alignment with Finance

We've covered most of the structural stuff, but there is a final one that affects organisations as well as the regions and the national picture. Even if we can get some workforce planning done at team level, at the same time finance are being asked for workforce figures linked to the financial picture that they have been submitting. As these processes are different, we either end up with different figures, or one ends up trumping the other. I don't think I've ever seen finance lose that one...

Solution: Obviously, having a single joined-up mechanism for providing workforce figures between operations and finance from the national level down would be the answer to this, but that does require a degree of honesty that might not be entirely palatable to all parts of the system. A solution that Manchester found as part of its devolution agenda was to show the various workforce future pictures together to start the conversation about whether the finance or the operations future, or a combination of the two, was more likely.

Scarcity of Workforce Planning Skills

The issues go beyond the structural and organisational. In the modern health and care system, workforce planning skills are scarce. Those skills used to be core for service managers, but years of increasing demand and a need to chase RTTs and waiting lists has led to the atrophy of skills just when they are most needed. In addition, there are a range of new system roles who haven't been trained, and greater need for these skills in areas like Primary and Community care.

Solution: We need an explosion of skills in front line staff: Service Managers, team leaders, STP, ICS and ICP management, regional teams, primary care Practice Managers, Care Home Managers etc. Core tools and approaches should be free and available, although given the scale of the challenge, if people want to use any one of the many approaches for which a fee needs to be paid, then so be it.

Not Enough Time and Resource

And we need the people, as even with the skills and the tools, people need time to be able to lead workforce redesign, and no-one has the time to focus on it (especially with all the barriers in the way). And even if we have the time to lead transformation, we need help from the analysts, the front-line staff need to inform the change, management need time to support it etc. Implementation of the changes, even if we have time to agree them, is going to further drain the time of the people on the ground, even though it is the answer. We're going to have to pilot, double-run in some cases and train and support new roles. It all takes time. This is time people don't have because, and you may have missed this earlier: We Don't Have Enough Staff.

Solution: We will have to carefully prioritise the changes, make changes quickly to prove success and create the new supply of roles to help address the demand. Engaging people throughout the process will be vital, because there is no way that this gets done without the continued goodwill of a workforce that always goes the extra mile or ten.

It Isn't Really Clearly Defined

Alright, that isn't strictly true. It is clearly defined, but it is a very wide topic, so that when people say, "workforce planning", they don't always mean the same thing.

Workforce planning can be defined, as it was by HEE earlier in this book. And as we discussed then it can include a whole range of skills across a wide set of timelines. Which explains why people might not all mean the same thing when they talk about it.

Solution: Knowing about these distinctions, when we engage in workforce planning, we always try to define which aspects of these we are talking about, to remove any confusion.

So, in summary it is practically impossible. But the reward for doing it, and the risks of not doing it, are too great not to try. So, let's get into it.

Chapter 1.4

Workforce Planning Skills

We have a wide range of topics to consider when we talk about workforce planning, and there are a lot of skills required. We won't cover all of this in the book, but we'll discuss the skills needed in six main areas of workforce planning. So, you still get your money's worth:

Operational Management: Day to day/ week to week management, scheduling and rostering.

Then there are three skills that make up the topic of redesign:

System Redesign: Designing the system around the workforce to optimise how people work in the system.

Workforce Redesign: This is the technical workforce bit, including the redesign of roles.

Modelling the Workforce: Sorting out the numbers.

Then the final two:

The Delivery Plan: Developing and implementing the actions to make the future a reality.

Infrastructure: Embedding people and workforce planning into the way the health and care system works.

Operational Management

Operational management workforce planning skills are those required for Service and Practice Managers, the largest element being the daily and weekly management, with some annual and a little strategic work.

Staff are focused on quality delivery, customer service, their team and meeting a budget, so training and development can focus on any and all of these.

Redesign

There are a few skillsets in here. First, system redesign. You can't redesign workforce in isolation of its place within the system. Before, or while, we consider our staffing model, we need to consider:

Process: How can we improve or simplify the process to adjust the impact on staff? How can we influence demand?

Digital: What new software and digital tools can we introduce? This could include a robot, care-coordination system or anything else that can help our teams meet the needs of service- users (or help them meet their own needs).

Estates and Equipment: Can we change where we deliver care? Can new buildings or equipment help?

Organisational Structure: Can we make life more efficient with fewer or more teams? In different organisations?

Considering all that together is system redesign.

On the specific workforce side we need to consider workforce redesign, including the introduction of new (or amended roles). This is based on an understanding of what the demand (patients and their conditions) is and how the individual roles can meet that.

Finally, we need to model those changes using our view of demand, supply and how they link together.

It's all very fun, which is why there are so many approaches and tools. If we take the whole topic of redesign, there are a myriad of approaches that can be taken. Most focus on system redesign but include workforce within it. Some, like CLEAR are workforce led, but are also system redesign methodologies. Others, like Six Steps are almost entirely focused on workforce. A longer list is included at the end of this section.

These approaches each have much to offer, but most are proprietary and need to be procured through their owner. I tend to use a generic, free approach that we call WRaPT: Redesign. This is an extension of the approach required for WRaPT workforce modelling. We also recommend HEE STAR in the area of redesign, as it is a great approach to identifying the priorities for redesign. I've worked with almost all of the other teams mentioned here and have been impressed with most. As I've said before, what matters is that we redesign workforce, not which approach we use.

This book focuses on pragmatic approaches to running projects through design and implementation, and one core skill set that really helps is the ability to be able to manage a redesign project. An understanding of what is needed through mobilisation, stakeholder engagement, redesign, benefits realisation and implementation will be invaluable throughout. The workforce redesign bit is actually quite a discrete piece of work within a wider landscape of a change project, and if you have excellent skills and experience in that, then you won't find workforce redesign challenging.

The Workforce Plan

Leaving the topic of redesign, another key element is the development of an actual plan. There are two key parts to this:

Developing the Measures or options for dealing with workforce shortages (normally***):*** One of the mechanisms for this is the consideration of the seven R's: *Recruitment*, *retaining* staff (when otherwise they might leave), getting staff to *return* to work, *replacing* staff (with AI for example) and *retraining* staff. Key among these is also *redesigning* processes to reduce the need and also *re-energising* (getting more through wellness, behaviours and values work).

The Writing of the Plan itself: How to go about developing a plan and pulling a document together.

Infrastructure and Engaging Support

Finally, the strategic STP or ICS end, which generally includes the integration of the plan and planning process within the operation of the STP and beyond. NHSI/E have produced a System Workforce Improvement Model (SWIM) which provides a maturity range for the management of workforce planning across a system, which you can use as a guide to this, but we will look at the skills required later in this book.

The development of workforce planning skills in a system requires at least a light workforce hub or collaborative to champion workforce within the STP, govern the process, develop the capacity and engage teams.

In summary, there are a range of skills that you might need in order to master Workforce Planning for your specific situation. This book will cover these skills in the rest of the sections, covering: Workforce Redesign, Workforce Planning, Developing Workforce Hubs and finally the range of operational skills needed for front-line teams.

Chapter 1.5

Developing Workforce Planning Skills

The approach I use to develop managerial and front-line team skills is the same across all the domains I operate in, including workforce planning.

I see development as a pyramid (or is it a tetrahedron?), with three elements on the base, and one at the pointy bit.

The three elements of the base are:

Building Capability and Capacity Through Training: Knowing how to do it is a basic part of doing something. But on its own it isn't enough. You also need the time to do it.

Tools and Techniques: Training needs a base approach to form a shared language for those doing it, and to provide something concrete to go back to when you haven't used your training for a while. If this can be augmented with a digital tool, then this is even better, hence our use of the WRaPT: Redesign Approach and Tool.

Embedding in Your Organisation: The first two are surprisingly easy. Now it jumps to 'very hard' very quickly, as you need to ensure that the approach is embedded into the organisation in which you work, otherwise you won't be able to start it, complete it or maintain it into the future. The approach builds in how this is going to be sponsored, maintained, refreshed and celebrated, to reduce the chance of failure or atrophy.

Then we get to the last one. Every pyramid needs a point, and in this case the point is actually doing something useful with all of the above. When I am developing the team, we work **together** on an actual project. Preferably this should be something really important to the organisation or system (because that really helps with embedding it into the organisation). Development is action-learning focused, but also predominantly coaching to help people actually succeed at using the approach, adding value and gaining confidence through that success.

It is worth bearing these aspects in mind as we go through the approach in this book.

When I train in workforce planning, I approach it in three ways for three different audiences:

Operational Workforce Planning

Generally designed for front-line managers (Practice Managers, Team Leaders, Service Managers etc), operational workforce planning focuses around developing the team, or core group of people that work together to deliver great outcomes to service-users.

The outcome for a project like this is the development of the team to produce a costed, future-proof, high-quality workforce model for each front-line team, that builds into an organisation-wide workforce plan and strategy that will actually make a difference to the organisation.

The project typically covers:

Training in redesigning the team using the Workforce Redesign approach, based on an understanding of activity (or demand), budget and the current team, among other things. It also includes training in how to maintain teams in the face of changing demand and availability over the year, using tools such as e-rostering.

Bringing in ***Tools and Approaches*** like

e-rostering, WRaPT, HEE STAR and Apex Insight or population health management tools like Sollis.

Developing Measures to be able to continually monitor benefits, variances to plan and rates of adherence to new approaches, and to intervene as needed.

Running the ***Project*** to deliver a new workforce model, budgets and workforce improvement plans for the organisation or team.

Pathway/Project Redesign

A pathway or project redesign programme is typically based around the improvement of a single service, and the development of a central or front-line group to redesign the workforce, process and attendant digital, equipment, organisational and estates infrastructure.

The outcome for a project like this is a clear new process, workforce plan, workforce model and implementation plan to bring a step change to the way that the process is being undertaken. This is a typical process engineering outcome, but with a focus on the workforce redesign and model. Development of skills in this area includes:

Training in redesigning the process using the WraPT: Redesign approach, based on an understanding of activity (or demand), budget and the current team, amongst many other things.

Bringing in ***Tools and Approaches*** like HEE STAR and WRaPT.

Developing Organisation or System Support like executive leadership and monitoring of delivery through a Programme Management Office (PMO).

Running the ***project*** to deliver a new workforce and process (or care) model, with attendant implementation plan and support structures.

Planning and Infrastructure

A planning and infrastructure development programme is focused on building an effective team from the system individuals in the ICS, ICP, STP etc), that will need to lead and co-ordinate workforce planning and redesign.

The outcome for this type of project is the development of a group of individuals into a team that has developed a coherent workforce plan and strategy for the system, and the infrastructure to implement and adjust it over time. The project typically covers:

Training in developing and implementing workforce plans, and building capacity and workforce infrastructure.

Bringing in ***Tools and Approaches*** like WRaPT, NHSI's SWIM and HEE STAR.

Working With the System to develop plans.

Embedding the delivery and continued development of plans within the system through a ***Workforce Collaborative,*** putting in place the infrastructure to allow its continued operation.

Just reading this book or undergoing training in workforce planning isn't enough. You will need to find the capacity to do the work, and have available tools and techniques to support it. Critically, you must embed this within the organisation or system. A great way of doing this whilst also giving you practice is to do it in a real project, like one of the three described here.

Focus: Workforce Redesign Approaches

There are a range of Workforce Redesign approaches to choose from. These include quick, two-workshop approaches like HEE STAR, through to the three to six month data-led clinical education programme of CLEAR. Most are workforce redesign approaches, but some like CLEAR and WRaPT also cover workforce-led system redesign. Others, like LEAN include workforce as part of their overall system redesign approach.

HEE Star	HEE CLEAR Clinically Led Workforce Redesign	Six-Steps (Skills for Health)
Population Centric (Gold Business Consulting)	WRaPT: Redesign	Recipe for Workforce Planning (HEE)
SWIPE (Whole System Partnership)	Calderdale Framework (Effective Workforce Solutions)	LEAN, 6-Sigma, Vitalsigns etc

SECTION TWO

WORKFORCE REDESIGN

This skill set within workforce planning is focused on the redesign of process, organisation, estates, equipment, digital solutions AND workforce to develop a new workforce model for the future.

As we have discussed, there are a myriad of approaches to workforce and system/ process redesign and transformation. And to be honest, I really don't mind what process you are actually following, as long as you follow a process and actually get something done. Each of the approaches differ in who it is aimed at, whether it is primarily process or workforce led, the extent it considers patient need or whether you look at the current or future state first.

The approach that we use for Workforce Redesign is the core WRaPT: Redesign approach, a generic, free-to-use approach that builds on the basics of project management, workshop facilitation and workforce redesign, as well as nicely helping you develop a workforce model which you can put into the WRaPT tool or your own Excel creation. When I say "we", it's time to introduce Amina and Fiona who jointly built this approach with me, and who use it alongside the WRaPT tool every day. They'll be adding their thoughts in as we go along, although they have been instrumental in writing much of this section.

It's a five-stage process, set out on the next page, which we will go through step by step, although you'll note that the diagram shows a circle rather than a linear process. That is because you need to be able to go back and forth between the stages regularly, and because you can play around with the order to some extent as well, especially with the steps within the stages. Just see this approach as a set of guidelines and useful ideas within a rough framework, that you can use on its own, or alongside other approaches used within your organisation or system.

In this section, we will take you through the five stages and their attendant steps. We'll be covering a lot in these chapters including a range of skills in role redesign, workshop facilitation, developing interventions, building models, writing business cases and describing SMART goals. There's quite a lot to get through...

Amina and Fiona's view

When we get involved in a workforce redesign project, we have to meet it where it is. That often means working on developing a future state, whilst feverishly working to strengthen the governance and understand the current state. If you get the chance, start with scope and mobilise and move clockwise - but even in a perfect project you'll find yourself occasionally going back to previous stages, or previous steps.

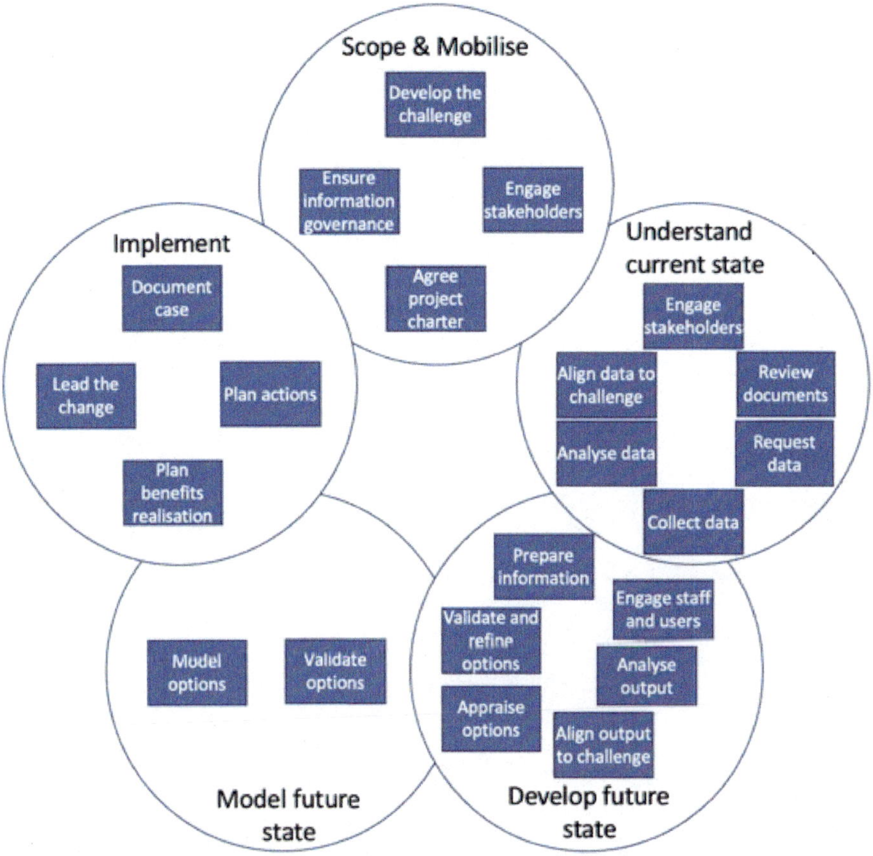

Diagram 1: WRaPT: Redesign Overview

Chapter 2.1

Scoping & Mobilisation

This first stage is one of five stages in the approach, and is in my opinion the most important. Mind you, we can talk about the first stage, but this is first only because you need to do some of this stuff right at the start, and the reality is that you need to keep coming back to this stage all the time.

Scoping and mobilisation is about setting the programme up to succeed at all stages. If I think about every project that I've been involved in that has gone wrong, it went wrong because the mobilisation wasn't done properly. And of course it wasn't done properly (because it is difficult to do) but you have to do it well, and keep it going well throughout the programme.

Getting started is a major struggle, because you need to get people to agree on what needs doing, and how they are going to help. And you want to get started on solving the problem, so there is a lot of temptation to get this stage out of the way quickly. Don't. Mobilisation needs to be done well. And to do it well, we cover the following four elements:

Amina and Fiona's view

It is as important to define what is out of scope as it is to define what is in scope. The one thing we know about the NHS, is that your project is not the only one that your organisation will be currently undertaking, let alone within your ICS or STP.

Having an overview of other projects being undertaken or the direction of travel of your organisation/ICS, will be helpful in describing the benefits of your project and understanding how outcomes of other projects/ programmes might affect the success of yours. There might be helpful overlaps that can be exploited, (such as data collection) or there might be unhelpful overlaps causing data collection fatigue, in which case you might want to think about increasing timeframes or considering other methods of collecting what you need.

Purpose

What are we trying to solve?

Why are we trying to solve it? What change is needed?

How do we know that we need to solve this? Are we sure that this is the problem that needs solving?

What is the impact of not doing it? What do we expect when we solve it?

Develop the Workforce Challenge that we are trying to address.

Engage Stakeholders in solving the challenge through this project.

Agree a Project Charter to give the project its structure.

Ensure Information Governance from the start of the project.

Developing the Workforce Challenge

We really need to know, in detail, what we are actually trying to solve and what solving it will look like. As with any project it is essential to determine and document a list of specific goals, deliverables, features, functions, tasks, deadlines and any associated costs.

The first part of this is developing a clear view on what we are trying to address, which we can do by considering:

- The purpose of the redesign.
- Its scope.
- Who needs to be involved.

The various highlighted lists in this section provide a helpful checklist of things to consider in each of these areas.

When developing the challenge, it's worth using SMART to define your goals. SMART stands for, as I'm sure you all know.

Specific: What exactly do you want to achieve?

Measurable: How can you tell that you have achieved it?

Achievable: Can it actually be done by you?

Relevant: Is it relevant to your skills, or does it directly benefit you?

Timely: By when will it be done?

So "I'm going to develop a workforce plan for the system", could become: "We're going to develop and recruit a workforce for the department that ensures that 95% of patients will be seen within four hours of arriving. We'll develop the plan by March and have the new staff in place by 2050". See - achievable...

Scope

What organisations, people, roles, services, patients, processes etc are in scope of the project?

Equally important - what is out of scope? What are we not going to include?

Where does the project start? What is its input?

Where does it end? What is the output?

Who Needs To Be Involved?

What stakeholders are needed for the steering group in order to ensure buy-in?

Who will be the chair of the steering group?

Who are the right representatives to get things done?

Who are the experts who will know what else is going on and help avoid duplication or the production of a different view?

What stakeholders do I need to include in the redesign?

Who are the experts that I need to get into the room?

Am I representing the diversity of my workforce, or the workforce I want?

Have I got enough Local Authority representation?

Have we involved the right service-users, their carers and volunteers?

Do we have representation from all providers?

What specialist contacts do I need to be involved? Information Governance? Data Providers? Estates? Digital?

Who is going to own the programme?

Who do we need in the team to deliver this? Programme Manager? Data Analyst? Session Facilitators, and people to maintain communication in between? Communications Experts? Modeller? Writer?

Who will this programme report to?

If you need more on SMART, look on the Internet as it's a well established approach.

Once you know what you are doing and who needs to be involved you can make a start in engaging people.

Engaging Stakeholders

The next job is to engage everyone. Realistically you have four groups, all of which will have their own engagement needs:

Amina and Fiona's view

We see a lot of projects that struggle to define their challenges as often they are not specific enough. There are techniques that can be used here like Root Cause Analysis. Sometimes you might see the symptoms, know you have a problem but not how to define it.

People say, "I'm struggling to recruit and that is my problem." This could be the challenge but it most likely is a symptom of the problem. What is the root cause? Is there actually a staff supply issue? If there is, then what can you do differently? Engaging people nearest to the problem can help you get a better understanding of the issues. Try to understand the wider picture: If it's a supply issue, is it local, national, global? What is being done to address this locally or nationally, or do we have to consider alternatives to overcome our challenge?

The Team: The people doing the actual work.

Steering Group: The people engaged in the programme but not actively doing the work.

Stakeholder Representatives: The people who will be engaged in redesign.

Stakeholders: All other people and groups who will be affected by the change.

The team and the steering group should be immediately engaged in a mobilisation event of some sort, to help complete the project charter and the governance documents, which I cover later.

The stakeholder representatives will also need to be engaged. You can combine this with the first step of the Current State stage, in which you engage stakeholders in what data and documents need to be collected and reviewed.

I won't go into too much detail on this, because this is more project management than workforce planning, but if you haven't done much project work before, you might find the below a useful set of steps for the initial engagement:

Develop a list of stakeholders.

Develop and communicate a standard set of information such as project explanation slides, a standard agenda and a list of what you need from them.

Book meetings.

Hold meetings.

Monitor and report on progress.

Document and agree outputs.

Follow up any agreed actions.

Pull outputs together and circulate learning.

Once you've had the initial discussions with the stakeholders, you need to consider how you maintain that engagement. And for that you need a communication plan.

To develop a communication plan, you first need to work out who most needs to be communicated with. So, list all your stakeholder groups or individuals and grade them based on how much influence they have and how interested they are.

People that are interested and influential need to be managed closely, with two-way engagement so that you can quickly react to their information and engagement needs. If they are influential but not interested, you need to ensure you are keeping them satisfied, so regular checks are needed, but you aren't going to person-mark them throughout. Interested people need to be kept informed, and the disinterested still need to be monitored, because they have some influence and some interest, so should not be ignored.

Amina and Fiona's view

When putting your stakeholder list together, don't forget Local Authority engagement. Much of our experience has been in health, rather than with local authorities, and that can lead us to unintentionally ignore their needs. In this case, one problem that can arise is that, because health is so fractured, workshops can be rammed with health staff, with one lonely person from the local authority. Can you balance that?

When bringing in providers, you also need to think about private providers. Private health and care providers, Primary Care Networks, care homes etc are all private providers, and you need to get a representative, and fair view, of needs in those areas.

To address this, we build it into a communication plan, which sets out the who, how, when, why and what of communication with various groups:

Who: Split the mass of stakeholders into groups (and individuals if they have high interest or high influence).

Why: What is the point of communication (ensuring they are informed? Getting their views? getting their help? All of the above?)

How: Determine how you are going to communicate:

- Broadcast: Regular email updates.
- Meetings: Engage through a discussion at an existing or new forum. Fora. Whatever.
- One-to-one Contact.
- Others: E.g. surveys to check engagement.

What: What are you going to communicate?

When: How often are you planning to communicate?

From then, all you need to do is to put that into a table and keep a log of communication so that you can see that it is being done, and make sure you aren't over or under-doing it. If you really want to go for it, you can keep a log of who is engaged etc., but I don't do that. For the simple reason that I don't keep notes on someone or write anything that I wouldn't want them seeing.I remember a colleague having a great time explaining to a client why they were identified as a "blocker" on a whiteboard left poorly cleaned in a room after a mobilisation meeting.

Developing Project Charter

This element requires the development and documentation of a charter that forms the basis for governance throughout the project. Other people call this a Project Initiation Document (PID). Whatever you call it, it should include key elements such as:

The Documented Question or challenge we are trying to address.

SMART goals.

Objectives and Benefits.

Project scope - what is in, what is out, where the project starts (input) and where it ends (output).

Roles, to identify who is doing what.

Plan and Timescales.

Terms of Reference for the ongoing monitoring/steering of the programme, including

- Chair (and deputy).
- What makes the meeting quorate?
- How will it be administrated: What is provided before the meeting, when and by whom. What information is collected, by when is it disseminated etc.
- Standard agenda.
- Objectives of the meeting.
- Who does it report to and how?

Googling "Project Initiation Document" will get you a range of versions. We use the WRaPT Project Charter document, which can be found at www.wrapt.org.uk. You can't click on that, this is a book...

Ensuring Information Governance

Oooh. Information Governance. If there is one thing that is going to extend your timescales, it's this little fella. I've known projects delayed by eighteen months because a health system couldn't sort this out.

Amina and Fiona's view

Bringing in patients can be tough, because you don't get to have a "behind doors" discussion. You can also get sidetracked if you have patients that focus on something that is very important for them, but may not be representative of the service-user group. For that reason, you might be tempted not to include service-users. Our advice is to always bring in a service-user view. We like to talk with project leads at the start to work out a way of bringing in a representative set of service-user views.

Project Information Governance is a term that means “the mechanisms by which information is going to be safely and appropriately used by the programme to meet its objectives”. That’s my definition (other definitions are available, always read the label).

Legally, we need to consider GDPR (EU General Data Protection Regulations), the Data Protection Act 2018, and any other legislation or toolkits that any party involved in the programme needs to adhere to or use, including the policies of each organisation.

Information Governance is complex because there are multiple sets of rules that need to be followed. Linked to this, the definition of many of these rules is based on varying degrees of risk appetite, meaning that there isn’t a one-size-fits-all approach.

You can add to that a general lack of understanding as to what it is, and the fact that those tasked with governing the organisation’s data have their own degrees of risk appetite, and varying amounts of time to devote to the subject. All this means that it is complicated and needs handling appropriately.

Luckily, this book is here to lead you through a few steps you should do at this first stage, which can make things a whole lot easier. Hopefully.

Get someone involved in the project right at the start who can advise on IG (Information Governance), highlight the main stakeholders and ensure that we are completing the right document.

Build an IG plan that covers the actions and timelines for:

- Agreeing requirements.
- Agreeing parties.
- Engaging IG leads in each organisation.
- Agreeing documentation.
- Completing documentation.
- Monitoring.

Agree your data requirements. This might evolve as you go through the stages, but we should consider:

- What workforce data do we actually need (personally identifiable data must only be collected with a fair purpose).
- Do we really need to know ethnicity, date of birth or sexual orientation? We might need such protected characteristics, we might not, so let's just be clear what we need and why when collecting data.
- What exact data fields do we need, and what are the systems we intend to get these from?
- What patient/activity data do we actually need?

Agree who is included in the agreement: Create a list of all of the parties to be involved in the data collection, processing and sharing, and the direction in which the data will flow.

Develop an IG engagement plan for the IG leads for each of the organisations in order to:

- Enlighten and engage them.
- Understand their requirements for documentation.

- Agree timelines and timescale.

- Build escalation route for the inevitable blockages.

Create a data sharing agreement: Develop documents that state the purpose and conditions for sharing the data as well as retention schedules, storage arrangements, review date and sign off.

Ensure that IG is part of the governance throughout the programme, checking that you are adhering to the agreements.

Prepare for breaches: If you are careful, you won't make them yourself, but others will – make sure that everyone knows that they should follow reporting processes when this happens.

In my first workforce project in the NHS (which was a very long time ago…), I was responsible for a data breach. I sent round a template, with an example line of data that I thought was made up, but it wasn't. It was the data for a real person and included home address, date of birth and lots of other data. One of the Trusts we sent the data request to spotted this and, following their process, informed us. When that came through, I felt absolutely sick, but we followed our process and raised it with our host trust. The person was told and offered support; the processes we used were checked; the Executive Lead was told; a plan was put in place so this wouldn't happen again. And that was it: No one shouted or screamed or even criticised and the organisation (and I) learned. If the person hadn't raised it, or if we hadn't put it through our process, no-one would have learned. So, every time we use data, I use that example in the hope that people won't be afraid to learn from their own mistakes. Or mine

So, at the end of this stage, you should have:

- Project charter, that sets out the issue, stakeholders, expected benefits and costs, roles, scope, timeline and milestones.
- Agreed governance.
- Stakeholder engagement plan.
- Information governance plan.

And you are ready to start collecting data...

Focus: Data

Before we get into too much more of the process, let's consider what sort of data we need to collect. What you collect depends on what you are trying to achieve. It could be the bare minimum for a WRaPT workforce model. It could just be workforce information, or it could include process, equipment, organisation, facilities and estate information. So, what might be included?

In general, there are four things to consider when pulling data together:

Quantitative facts about what is going on: There should be no doubt about this information as facts are facts.

Qualitative thoughts such as known issues and strengths: These can be ideas and opinions.

Good practice examples: Suggested by the team, or from the document review (including HEE STAR).

Expectations on how things will change: Anything to do with what will change before any future model becomes a reality.

...and a whole list of things you could consider bringing together.

As I said, you should pick what you need depending on the question you are trying to answer, but it is likely that you will want information in four groups:

Workforce: Information related to the staff doing the work

Activity: Anything to do with the patient or service-user.

Drivers: The information needed to link activity to the workforce that does it.

Other: Information about the process, digital, organisation, estates etc.

Examples of what you might like to collect in each area is set out on the final pages of this section.

Let's consider a few topics related to data, starting with the concept of "drivers".

Activity

The collection of activity data is often one of the most difficult aspects of workforce planning, yet it is arguably the most important. When we are talking about staff, we know what we are talking about – but activity can be much more complex.

First, we need to consider the difference between demand and activity. Demand is based around the actual needs of the patients or service-users. Activity is the translation of that into what walks through the door and gets treated or helped. If you only have enough staff to service twenty customers per day, activity will be twenty per day. But that is not the demand, which could be ten times that level.

The gold standard for demand information in health and social care is Population Health Management information. This approach involves looking at the wider determinants of health of the population to provide real demand information that can be used to drive transformation in models. By its nature it requires much more of a population response, because it unearths considerably more real demand for health and care.

Secondly, activity can be set at different levels. You can record it at total levels (e.g. bed days), or you can record activities more granularly at a sub-activity level. You can record it as contacts, or break it down into the types of contacts.

I like to try to keep things as simple and general as makes sense, but as complicated as you need in order to be able to analyse by role, and to engage your audience. Just telling your audience that the team handle 20,000 contacts per year is interesting, but it doesn't give us much information. How many of these contacts are for the same person? How many are complex? Do they need different skills to handle and process them? Or need different approaches? If so, we'd be better off breaking them down to condition. The CLEAR approach does this really well, engaging clinicians in designing new workforce models in response to new insights from activity data.

Finally, how long are we collecting it over? It doesn't really matter as long as it is consistent, but we tend to consider something on an annual basis. This allows us to consider rarer events, alongside the day to day, but when we work annually, we need to realise that not every week or day within that will be the same.

Drivers

What we call "driver" information is anything that links activity and workforce. By linking workforce to activity, we can undertake a lot of the analysis that is vital to the modelling of the future:

You can adjust efficiency up or down and see the impact on staff numbers.

You can change the person who does it.

You can see the impact on staffing of removing or streamlining steps.

A way to record this is on a table with roles down the left, activities across the top, and noting the % of each role's time spent doing each activity, hopefully adding up to 100%.

This approach uses percentages, which is how the WRaPT tool does it. But there is an alternative, as you can just record how much time people spend on each activity. So, instead of saying "we spend 50% of our time working on inpatient appointments", you can say, "I spend an hour on each inpatient appointment".

Either is fine, but both have risks. Years of experience has shown us that the percentage approach has fewer risks, but the timed one is the most flexible and the one best used by experts. An even better approach is to do both, and then compare them...

Fixed and Variable

Almost everyone has fixed and variable tasks in their role. Variable tasks only happen when there is activity, whereas fixed tasks are done no matter how much activity you have. You can also add fixed-variable tasks, which do change with activity levels, but not in a linear fashion (but it is simpler to see these as variable).

If you include fixed tasks, you are essentially reducing the amount of staff time that is available. If 50% of your job is fixed, you have only ½ FTE to deliver the 1000 activities.

If you assume all tasks are variable, then you calculate things differently. In this case, you have one FTE to deliver the activity, but you take longer to do each one, e.g. one FTE to do 1000 activities.

Budget Versus Reality

One aspect of data that needs special attention is the relationship between reality, budget, what has been commissioned and what the staff establishment is. Activity, workforce and service levels can all be considered against these four different aspects:

Reality: What activity is coming through the door? What staff do we have? What service levels do we provide?

Budget: What activity level is our budget set for? What staff is it set for?

Establishment: What staff do we have as our establishment?

Commissioned: What activity are we commissioned to deliver? At what service level? Are we commissioned for a specific number of staff?

Collecting this information allows us to do some very simple and effective analysis, and ensures that we are collecting a consistent set of data.

Collecting a Data Set for a Workforce Model

Proper workforce planning needs a workforce model of some sort. Whether it is something in WRaPT, or something more complex in Excel, you need some basic information to make a workforce model:

Workforce: Hierarchy information (organisation, team etc), role, title, grade, number, salary and cost centre.

Activity: Activity name and number.

Drivers: % of their time each person takes on each activity.

With these three, you have all you need to develop a model (which we'll cover in the session on modelling later).

What Data to Collect for a Full Current State Analysis

Using the word "full" there might be a little risky, but the list on the next two pages should keep you busy enough.

Workforce - Quantitative

- Numbers in each role
- Grades
- Salary/costs +/- on costs
- Sickness rates
- Budget
- Recruitment history
- Joiners/leavers - staff turnover
- Age profile
- Morale/staff survey results
- Staff rotas and job plans
- Roles breakdown
- Skills, behaviours and attitudes needed
- Bank and agency spend
- Overtime

Workforce - Good Practice

- New roles
- Models
- Safe levels

Workforce - Qualitative

- Exit interview results
- Issues faced by staff

Workforce - Changes

- Expected turnover
- Recruitment plans

Activity - Quantitative

- Population/need
- Actual activity
- Patient experience

Activity - Qualitative

- What issues do we face?
- Ideas for handling demand differently

Activity - Other

- Benchmarking
- Activity & demand projections

Drivers

- Quantitative: % of time each role spends on each activity
- Qualitative: Ideas for improvement
- Good practice: Benchmarking and other models

Other - Quantitative

Organisation

- Org charts

Process

- Process maps
- Schedule of opening hours
- Service offer/ specification and contract
- Diaries

Technology

- Digital tools

Equipment

- Equipment lists

Estates

- Company location/maps
- Staff locations
- Patient/service-user locations

Other - Qualitative

- Issues we face
- Strengths we have
- Ideas for improvement

Other - Changes

- Technology predictions
- Planned system changes

Other - Good Practice

- PESTLE analysis
- SWOT analysis
- Other models

Focus: Health Education England's Star Tool

The HEE Star tool was developed to support workforce transformation, helping providers understand their workforce requirements and also providing a range of potential solutions. It can be used to support you to have productive conversations about the challenges your system faces and an accompanying online directory signposts to over 300 opportunities, products and resources available through HEE to help design solutions to the challenges.

It's use is entirely consistent with the approach used in this book, with CLEAR and all other workforce redesign approaches.

For more information, search HEE Star online.

Chapter 2.2

Understanding the Current State

This stage is about building an understanding of what is going on at the moment. It represents a baseline, a position from which we can build the future state. In the WRaPT: Redesign approach, you start with a baseline, develop a future state, and then move from one to the other.

In later sections we'll consider different types of baseline, but no matter what sort you are pulling together, you follow a similar process:

- ***Engaging stakeholders*** to identify what data we need, where we can get it and how we should collect it.
- ***Reviewing documents*** that can provide us with the information we need to start.
- ***Requesting data***, in a sensitive and planned manner.
- Directly ***collecting data.***
- ***Analysing*** what you have found.
- ***Aligning data to the challenge***, and checking it with stakeholders.

You may well have to complete elements of each of these tasks multiple times. And whilst, like any element of WRaPT: Redesign, you can pick where you start, for the best results you should begin and end with engaging the stakeholders.

Engaging Stakeholders

The stakeholders in the process are two things: They are experts, and they are people that have a stake in the current and future process. In both cases, you need to treat them with the respect that they deserve. They can not only give you excellent information, but they also need to feel involved in the process if you are to have any chance of developing a good new model (and getting it implemented and maintained).

Right at the start then, you need to find out how to go about data collection in the environment you are in, asking for information such as:

What documents or data that already exist do you suggest we look at? Where can we get them ?

What data would you find useful/would you need to be able to undertake redesign? Who would have that?

Who are the best people to contact with a data request? Would you be able to help by sending an introductory or chase email?

We normally use the following approaches to direct data collection: Is there anything we should be aware of? Good people to talk to?

Is there any analysis of information you would find useful?

At the end, it is really about checking in to make sure you have done it right.

We have collected this information: What do you think? Does it look right? Have we missed anything?

Does this analysis look right?

In total, it is about ensuring that they are bought into the process, building on and not ignoring their expertise to create the best outcome.

Reviewing Documents

The next step is to review the documents that are suggested and others that you can locate through various sources. Other documents can be found on the Internet, or on HEE STAR.

Recording and integrating findings from a mass of documents, can be quite tough. We typically use a table to record findings, cutting and pasting relevant text and bringing it together in one place with appropriate metadata (source, author, date etc).

Requesting Data

Ah yes, data requests. Have any of you ever received a data request? If so, then when it falls to you to send one, all you need to do is to think about what you would have wanted before inflicting one on someone else. Consider, which one of these would you prefer:

Version 1: "You must fill in this ten page spreadsheet now"; or

Version 2: "Can I please help you to complete this…

…reasonably sized data request…

…which we need to complete because…

…which will help you because…

…and we will keep centrally so you'll not be asked again…

…can you suggest where we can just get this from, or if you already have anything similar."

Amina and Fiona's view

When looking at data needs, spend some time first looking at what data is available publicly and then build the data request from there.

There's loads out there via NHS Digital, NWID, ONS, QOF (see glossary). Many are available via a quick Internet search.

Some sites you might have to register for, but we've not generally come across a problem with getting access.

Alright, the second way might be just a bit much, but you see where we are going with this. A data request should appreciate that the person probably doesn't have to fill this in if they don't want to, and is probably busy, so being pleasant about it is a good idea, as is letting them know what is in it for them

It should only collect what we need so it's all about keeping it tight rather than a fishing expedition, - and it should be co-ordinated with others where possible to avoid duplication of effort before or after. Finally, it should offer help, rather than it just being an 'ask'.

Data requests are a nightmare unless they are handled right. Other key things to consider are:

Can you go in person rather than just sending by email so that you can make a human contact, explain why you need it and answer any questions?

Contract with the person to send the data by a certain time. You can't just send an email and expect it to be done, as they have promised nothing.

Develop your governance at the start:

- What is your plan for engagement and chasing?
- How will you track progress?
- Who will you escalate to, and how are you engaging with them to make sure that they help straight away?

Directly Collecting Data

So, you can request data, but just doing that is probably not a great idea. It is better to collect data directly for at least four reasons:

1) You can gain a degree of control over collection that data requests don't always give you. If you go in person, you know that you are going to get something;

2) Engaging with people in their real-world environment will help you build relationships for the later re-design;

3) By getting on the ground, you can check that the data you've been given makes sense, so risk having fewer problems (and looking less of an idiot) when you come to check it with stakeholders; and

4) It is much more fun and interesting...

And there are many fun and exciting ways that you can go about such direct data collection. So you get some variety as well.

Options include:

Interviews: The old standard way of getting information, sitting down and chatting with people, preferably at their place of work if pandemics allow. It is a great way to build relationships, get information and check your learning. If you do one piece of direct data collection then this is the one to do.

Time & Motion Study: I practically grew up doing these, and they are surprisingly fun things to do. Basically, you follow people round, building up a picture of the tasks they do and the time it takes to do them, which you can do with a stopwatch if you want to come across as particularly professional.

Process Review: By combining elements of time & motion study and interviews, a full process review can allow you to build a full picture of process, skills needed, skills used, equipment and digital tools used, locations and more.

Diaries: Some people you talk to are more than happy to make quick and confident estimates of how they spend their day. Some people are much less happy about giving even the slightest bit of a clue as to how they spend their time, like it's some sort of puzzle or state secret. If people find it difficult to provide this information, then asking them to keep a diary of their day and week can be a mechanism to collect it. I'm not a big fan of this, as you are asking people to spend time collecting data but it's sometimes worth trying.

Workshop: Interviews and process reviews can take a lot of time, so you can run a data collection event to bring everyone together. It's time efficient, engaging and can bring together everyone's views in one agreed place. You can run a very quick project with a single data collection and one follow up redesign workshop.

Survey: Surveys can be a great way to collect data because you can get a lot of information quickly, in a format that allows for quantitative data collection which can be great for presentation. I like to use a survey as a step after collecting some initial data because you can use it as a way to collect more data, to check the data you have, to get a view on how many people agree with it, to prioritise, to engage and to have something to present. Not bad when tools like SurveyMonkey cost you nothing…

Analysing Your Findings

No-one needs to see every bit of data you have found. You can usefully draw some conclusions from this and present it as information. You also don't need to do this all on your own as you can engage other stakeholders to do it with you to build up that all important buy-in and make sure you aren't making any errors.

Helpful analysis might include:

Demand Analysis: Building an interactive view of demand or activity using a Population Health Management System (like Sollis) or a visual package like Tableau This can then be used to look at specific groups or conditions so you can see where they've come from, what their condition is, where they move to etc.

Amina and Fiona's view

Once you have your data together for your baseline, set some time aside to review it with your stakeholders. If you have a deadline in mind, work backwards from the date and allow sufficient time for this step. We once presented a model to the Clinical Lead which was due to be included in a report that day. When we went through the model to validate it, we found that what we had been given for the current position was actually the aspirational future state numbers…

Workforce Model: Either in an on-line tool like WRaPT, or in an Excel model, or both, developing a model of links between data like activity and workforce can aid in analysis before, during and after the engagement workshops.

Sankey diagrams: To show the flow of activity between units, picking out large and small flows through a process. If you haven't seen these before, have a look on the Internet. They can be quite effective mechanisms for engagement.

Rich process maps: Detailed process maps including information like skills and volumes.

Organisation charts: Showing how many and what sort of staff are in each organisation and team.

Staff location maps: Showing where everyone works.

Service-user maps: Showing patient satisfaction at various process steps or at various activity levels.

Patient locations: Map of patient density by postcode.

Reality versus commissioning versus budget: Analysing the differences between them.

This step is all about the use of analytics to take data, create actionable information and engage clinicians, managers and others by creating a story.

Aligning Data to the Challenge

Finally, you need to align the data back to the challenge. Like all these steps, this is something that you should realistically be doing with every bit of data you collect. There are three things to consider:

Is it enough? Do we need more data now that we have learned what we have learned?

Is it accurate? How can we be sure that it was accurate originally, and that we have processed it properly?

Has it been validated? Have we checked with the stakeholders?

Once you have a full set of data, you are ready to design the future state, using what you have learned to drive it.

Amina and Fiona's view

It's helpful to remember that a baseline is a great starting point for a discussion, even if you are worried about inaccuracy or lack of agreement. If people disagree, or have more information, we can validate it and update the baseline. Don't let these worries put you off pulling together a current state picture or as best a version as you can. We never cease to be surprised at the impact a baseline picture has in terms of presenting things that should be obvious, and in focusing conversations on facts.

By the end of this step, you should have:

- Evidence of the document review.
- A clear baseline of data and information.
- An understanding of your current state .

As we said at the start, this can be useful in its own right, but the next stage of our journey is to do something with it....

Chapter 2.3

Developing the Future State

The future state, perhaps rather unsurprisingly, sets out the results of the planned transformation. In WRaPT: Redesign, it takes the current state and transforms it into its planned new state. In other models, like Six-Step, the development of the future workforce state practically starts the process. I like to understand the current first, but I can also see the attraction of the blank sheet of paper approach, as it is unfettered by the restraints of the present. I just prefer to understand what I am transforming.

The future state stage includes:

Prepare information on the current state with which to engage the redesign.

Engage staff and users in developing the change and future state through a workshop or similar approach.

Analyse output of the workshops and transformation.

Align output to challenge to ensure that it meets the brief.

Appraise options for benefits.

Validate and refine options with stakeholders.

Future State Skills

The trouble with developing a future state, is that it tends to need a lot of different skills to do it well. This is not easy stuff, but luckily, you don't need to do it alone, and can pull in skills from others to deliver it.

The skills that you need specifically for the future state development can be split into four key groups:

General redesign: These include process mapping, facilitating a workshop and project management. Remember when we talked about the balance between workforce redesign and system redesign? Unless there is a redesign project going on alongside it that you can be a part of to do the workforce bit, then you will need some basic redesign skills:

- This will generally include a workshop of some sort, so you need to be able to present and facilitate a workshop or find someone to help.
- You have to do at least some basic process step mapping, and attach workforce data to it.
- You will need basic time and project management skills. This is a range of skills in reality, many of which you will certainly already have, and if you want to improve these, there are many courses out there.

Workforce redesign: Specifically for workforce, there are two skill groups that we will cover in this book. These are at the absolute core of workforce redesign:

- Role redesign: There are a range of approaches to this, but all of them share a common set of attributes that we will discuss here. The basic aim is to build the best set of roles for the staff, for the service-users and the organisation
- The Seven R's: It's all very well redesigning roles, but that is only part of the solution. The other thing that you need to plan with the group is how you are going to fill the workforce gaps. We will go over the Seven R's: Recruit, retain, retrain, return, replace, re-energise and redesign.

Workforce modelling: You will need some basic workforce modelling skills to record the future state and options. You have some choices for this, but ones we use tend to be:

- ***WRaPT:*** The web-based tool for workforce modelling. Whilst it has a user-guide and is quite easy to navigate in its core functions, building the skills to quickly build a baseline and scenario models is worth the time. If you are able to use the tool to answer questions in real time it can be a great part of workshops, as questions can be asked, answered and then built on to generate an agreed model right there in the room.

  Whether you build that level of skill or not, workforce modelling skills are a useful part of your arsenal.

- ***Excel etc:*** You don't have to use WRaPT. If you are an Excel whizz, or want to model other things, you can use different software. You may want to play with activity and show how you got to the aggregated activity numbers that are in WRaPT. You may want to break down actions into lots of different steps, so that you can play with team level actions. Or we may want to provide a standard model that anyone with excel skills can use.

Planning: There are two other skills that you need for a future state that may not be part of a workshop or redesign process:

- Planning process: The building of a plan can be on many different scales, from the largest national people plan, to an operational plan for a practice or specialty team. The amount of time that this takes can also vary even within the different levels of complexity. The skills needed here are running workshops, being able to prioritise, being organised etc.

- Writing a plan: Finally, writing the plan down is critical, because we need to communicate it for agreement and to identify responsibilities – and we need to track its implementation. You may need to complete a business case, a presentation for a group or document a one hundred page plan for a national audience. Later, we will look at what is needed to develop the actual output of all this workforce planning.

Development of the Future State

The fundamentals of this step are to assess the feasibility of what can be developed in conjunction with the knowledge of your context and current state (aligning data and research). We need to work out what we can feasibly do, based on our knowledge of the

Amina and Fiona's view

WRaPT is a versatile tool, which is very easy to use.

Most of the modelling that you do in Excel can actually be done in WRaPT but of course you might just want to show it differently or might just be more comfortable playing with Excel.

But as a word of warning, we have found that not every managers has been completely comfortable with Tableau or Excel, and how many errors sneak in.

current and the possible. As we have said before, workforce transformation and redesign is part of overall transformation and redesign, so we will need to consider quite a bit.

In health and care at the moment we are probably going to be talking about the transformation of services. Obviously, good planning every year would see a constant evolution of services, but the reality is that that is rarely achieved and so we have a massive backlog of change to address. So, let's break down the three levels of transformation:

New models of care: We need to understand if there is already a new model of care for the area. In reality, workforce seems to lead the debate here, but as we have said before, there cannot be complete workforce redesign without covering the other areas: Will workforce redesign be supported by a change in process, in organisation structure, in estates and equipment or in technology?

Then we are into the ***workforce redesign*** itself. Here, we may generate new roles, amend the work of existing roles or extend roles to be able to do more or different things.

Finally, ***redesign actions.*** What else needs to transform to actually make all this stuff work? What needs to change so that we can grow our own staff to fill positions, to build leaders, to ensure that this is a great place to work? What will be the new training and development for people? How can we release time to care?

Amina and Fiona's view

There are three sides to any task: cost, quality and time. We argue that you can write a plan in a day, it's just that the quality will suffer. We once worked with a system to develop a short plan quickly, and then later developed this into a much larger and more detailed plan, in response to changing stakeholder needs.

A complete new future state will consider all of these potential elements.

Right, that's enough of that, now onto the six steps in this stage. Not the Six-Steps approach by Skills for Health, the six steps in this stage. Blimey, this is getting unnecessarily confusing…

Step One: Preparing the Information

The key to a good redesign workshop is in two types of preparation. The first, is preparing the people (which we will discuss under engagement). The second, is preparing the information. We break this down into four areas:

Highlight the issues: Why are we changing/what do we need to solve? You can add in here things like, what are we good at? What do we need to keep?

Build the "story": All the data that you have collected has helped you get to this point, but it is pointless to just bombard everyone with all of it. We have found that it is useful to set out to people what you have researched, what you have discarded and what you have brought to the group, so including a bit of the story of the data collection is a good start.

Consider what the answers might be: You can go into a workshop with no idea of what the answer might be. That is fine. But if you have drawn some conclusions from the work, then you can present a set of findings that people can amend, add to, prioritise and respond to.

Prepare some draft options for consideration: ...and if you have come up with some findings, you can draw your own conclusions and take it to the option stage. The aim of the workshop is not to rubber-stamp your views, which generally never actually brings anything to implementation, even if you get out of the room with your views intact. The aim is to allow the combined wisdom of the group to develop the options. But the more you know about the way it could go in the session, and the pro's and con's of each, the better able you are to respond to options presented and to take people to the next step.

Step Two: Engaging Staff and Users

So, then we are into the engagement stage. This is where you need a whole host of skills from our list. And this is where you are probably going to want to run a workshop (or workshops), as no single approach is better than bringing people together to go through the redesign process. You don't have to do it through a workshop, but I can't think of a single time where I redesigned roles without one.

Who to Engage in a Workshop?

To do this requires stakeholder engagement. The majority of these will be the people identified right at the start of the process, as many will be operational and can therefore identify

Amina and Fiona's view

This is my favourite part of the work as building and presenting a picture of workforce is always popular and helps people quickly see where issues are. Something as simple as a chart showing the age profile of staff, or a map showing how many people are at each site, can unlock discussion. We first show these to the steering group, as it is sometimes the first concrete piece of workforce analysis they have seen.

potential future state options and any limitations.

You need to check a few things when pulling your list together:

Who are the experts I need to get in the room?

Am I representing the diversity of my workforce, or the workforce I want?

How can I get care providers involved? I come from a health background, so often forget to include the care part of the equation. On top of that, health provision is so fractured, that workshops can be rammed with health staff, with one lonely person from the local authority.

How to you get a balanced patient or service-user view? Bringing in patients can be tough, because you don't get to have a "behind doors" discussion, but they bring a clear view of what the service-user needs (if you get a suitably representative group).

How can you fairly represent private providers? Primary Care Networks, care homes etc, are all private providers, so how do you get a representative, and fair view, of needs in those areas?

What stakeholders will have credibility when it comes to bringing in the rest of their group/colleagues?

Who do we need to include? Workshops could include a whole host:

- Clinicians (from all sectors of health)
- Expert social care deliverers
- Managers
- Patients / Patient Groups
- Volunteers
- Carers
- Commissioners
- Education Providers
- Unions / Staff Side
- 3rd Sector Providers
- ICS Leads
- Private Providers
- Local Authority
- Primary Care
- HR
- Estates
- Finance
- IT
- Transformation Leads
- Business Analytics
- Professional Bodies
- NHSI/E, HEE etc

How many workshops do I need? This again depends on what you want to achieve. You could have one large workshop or, some smaller ones, and follow up with a large one? Or hold a small one first to get some options, then include a bigger group? It's up to you and your steering group to define how to get the right outcome.

Facilitating a Workshop

Facilitating a workshop is a set of skills in its own right, and is a set that is worth developing. To help with that, we'll pick out some important elements for running a workshop over the next two pages, but more in-depth development in this area will pay dividends.

First, if the first time that you engage with everyone is at the workshop, you are going to have a really hard time. Make things easier for yourself by talking and engaging with people before it, because:

You will learn about the people in the room: Who is going to be difficult or enthusiastic?

You can reflect back what you have heard, and thus build consensus.

People will be more comfortable with you and less likely to be challenging to your facilitation role.

Second, send out the agenda, and make sure that people know why they are there. This helps you to address any "I thought we were here to discuss something else" challenges. The agenda for the session can follow any path, but we recommend that you include:

Welcome and introductions: Avoiding the creeping death of everyone introducing themselves if it is a big group. We tend to get people to introduce themselves to their tables and get someone to report back on who is on each table.

Background: Get a sponsor to present on why we are here and what we aim to do. It is also worth getting a service-user to provide their view on why it is important.

Understanding the baseline: Present the current state so that people can identify the strengths and opportunities for change.

Session on identifying solutions: This will be the main part, and will focus on the redesign.

Prioritising the identified solutions.

Action planning: This is something you need to watch. In my experience, you want to avoid asking people at the end who is going to do what as it wrecks the energy. Think about a Hollywood film: They tend to start quite light and with all going well, then it gets tough in the middle, and then finally the good guys win. Introducing sudden energy-sucking volunteer hunting at the end will just bring the mood down. It might be worth saving that for session two...

Third, you need to think about:

What do I want to get out of this workshop? A tough workshop where you get progress is better than an easy workshop without achieving your goal.

Plan the breaks (and food/drinks).

Who needs to be there?

Does anyone have any roles? Table facilitators for example?

How do we win this workshop and get what we want out of it? Are there things we need to do to increase the chance of success?

How are we writing this up? Table notes, post-its and flipcharts need to be quickly written up and synthesised. We need to know who is doing that and how, or we will just lose it all.

Next, this won't just be one workshop. To gain consensus, you will probably need to do multiple workshops, and maintain constant communication in between.

Finally, we also need to go back to that point about people being people and human. There are some things that people think are going to happen that will be bad for them. They don't know how they will cope. There are even some, that ask why we should change at all. These people will behave in variable ways, which it helps to be aware of.

I'm not going to go into a lot of detail on how to facilitate behaviours as courses on facilitation are available on-line and through a range of providers. I do, however, want to flag three key things:

Number One: Look out for bad behaviours in a workshop. I'm sure you can all think of people that have behaved in at least one of these ways in a workshop:

- Rambling or taking up too much time.
- Argumentative.
- Dominating or shutting out the views of others.
- Holding side conversations.
- People that are wrong and that introduce wrong information as if it were true.

It is your job to get the best agreement on the best solution you can to address the issues, so you need to address these behaviours.

Facilitation can be lonely, but it shouldn't be, because everyone else in that room should also be focused on the same thing. Expect and ask for help from the group.

Number Two: A few good tactics for poor behaviour that tend to work for me are:

Amina and Fiona's view

The redesign workshop is the toughest part of workforce redesign. Ensuring that you have a good set of well-briefed facilitators is key, as is ensuring that there is enough time to explore the issues and solutions, rather than rush through a packed agenda.

- Firm, but friendly confrontation. You've got to identify and call out behaviours.
- Non-verbal signals, like moving closer to gain attention for people that are taking too much time, etc.
- Reinforcing good behaviours with praise. Most people like a bit of praise, and the lack of it can be censure in itself.
- Private discussions. Just taking the person to one side and explaining their impact on the group can help.

Number Three: Have an approach in mind. There are key steps to a workshop that run from proposing through to deciding. You need to get the people through those steps, and you can call out when people are taking you backwards and thus not helping to get towards the goal.

In the end, you are there to get the best outcome that you can. You win only when you do that, and every time you do that. The actual outcome is also down to the humans in the room, and you can't account for all of this!

Workshop – Gaining Agreement Over Time

Your job is to gain as much agreement as possible. As we said, that doesn't necessarily have to happen in one workshop. We looked at stakeholder mapping earlier, and here we need to really gain agreement from those with high interest and high influence, either directly or through others.

Others will need to be kept informed or satisfied throughout. Others don't need to be influenced in between, but they can impact others, and they are stakeholders themselves, so you should monitor them and engage as necessary.

Workforce Redesign in Workshop

Right. Process redesign. Let's look at a simple process as an example of one that can be redesigned, or have its workforce redesigned:

- A referral is received and reviewed.
- If it is urgent then someone else reviews the referral to see if it is simple or not.
- If it is simple then a GP clinic is held, admin is handled and the process ends.
- If it is complex then it is sent to a tertiary provider.
- If it is non-urgent then a nurse clinic is held, admin is handled and the process ends..

So what other information would we find useful if we are going to do some workforce redesign on this?

Who does each step?

What skills are needed for each step?

What is the frequency?

What is the likelihood of each outcome from a decision point?

Where does the input come from?

What are the outputs (and where do they go)?

How long does each step take? Which you can combine with frequency to get a view on the overall scale.

Just basic process redesign can have an impact on workforce. You can remove steps that are unnecessary, reduce handoffs, replace tasks or reduce demand. Any or all of these can be used to change the staffing requirements straight away. But what we are really here for is workforce redesign.

How do you do role or workforce redesign from here? Well, you won't be surprised to hear that there are lots of ways of doing it. The Calderdale approach does this in detail really well, as does the Population Centric approach. Other approaches like Lean do this as part of a wider look. I've worked with at least five different specific methods including:

Functional Job Analysis: The data, people skills, and things required to do the work are recorded.

Task Inventory: The tasks are identified and for each task, the importance, time spent, and frequency are recorded.

Job Element Method: The characteristics of excellent performers are identified to give a more worker-oriented view.

Narrative task: Require interviews with the goal of creating a story that explains the key activities.

Critical incident technique: This focuses on what makes outstanding performance (either in a good or bad way) and evaluates the context, behaviours, and consequences of those behaviours. The goal here is to come up with behavioural best-practices.

In reality, these all do three things:

- *Analyse the actual tasks that are being done.*
- *Rate how important they are.*
- *Identify what skills are needed.*

And so we can add some more data to that which we've already collected as part of process review:

What is needed to do the step? What equipment, information, digital

Amina and Fiona's view

Facilitation really should be a team effort, and you can help by seeing yourself as a coach rather than as the star player. It isn't actually your job to create the future state: It is to help the group to develop the future state. There could be conflict over data and solutions, which is also not your problem as a facilitator, it's the group's problem, so you must make it clear that they are the ones that need to help solve it.

resources, skills, attitudes, etc. Whatever makes sense for the redesign.

What is excellent delivery? What does doing this step right really mean?

What is the story of this work? Where does this fit in the "narrative" of the work? To be honest, this is one I never do, but it might appeal to some people.

What is the consequence of good or bad action? What does doing this well (or badly) mean to other steps, to other staff or to service-users.

What makes this a great role for the person doing it? Supervision? Challenge? Development?

Using the redesign approaches from different lenses helps us to make a range of changes to roles.

In reality, we can do a few things:

We can change the skill mix: Typically moving skills up or down a hierarchy through role substitution. We often call this "operating at top of licence".

We can widen the job: Bringing together functions that were done by others and do them together.

We can simplify the role: Reducing the amount of tasks to create one that can be done by less qualified people, or can be done more efficiently.

We can deepen the role: Creating a richer role by giving people more responsibility or more development opportunity.

We can create whole new roles: These need to be designed so as not to be "add-ons".

And you need to think beyond the process. When things change, people might also want to consider:

Remuneration: Banding and salary

How they will be supervised: (And the additional time for that supervision).

Training needed.

What the career route is: This is very important due to potential short careers. For example, the clinical career for a mental health nurse can be short, as there are fewer clinical paths to choose than their physical health counterparts.

What makes this role excellent?: And how can this be demonstrated?

What volumes will they be expected to cover?

Job description.

What their process responsibilities will be.

Other things that make the job attractive.

How we build them into the budget or establishment.

How we communicate this role to others.

The reality of redesign is that there are more redesigns than there are implementations. It is possible that, for many legitimate reasons, the project will go little further than the workshop. Attention moves onto other things, people get asked to do other jobs, projects run out of resource or time, and they just stop. So, one thing that is worth introducing to any workshop is, what my friends at General Electric used to call "no regrets" projects. If someone can introduce or try something now, without recourse to higher powers, then we should identify, record, monitor and celebrate the success of very short-term improvement ideas

When we get to implementation we will talk about Kotter's steps for success in implementation. One of these is the need to create short-term wins. So, even at this design stage, we can actually implement small improvements, and in doing so perhaps help the whole redesign.

Step Three: Analyse Output

Once you've done your workshop or workshops, you need to build on it.

Align back to the challenge: Revisit your challenge statement and check that your proposed future state is going to solve the problem. Also, you need to sense check your assumptions.

Understand the impact of the redesign for use in the benefits realisation.

Undertake a formal impact assessment on patients, staff, communities, protected groups etc

Understand the shifts in workforce and activity: Undertake a gap analysis between the Current and Future states and setting out the change required.

This might then need another workshop, if it just isn't fitting. If you have a known gap in GPs, and the answer coming back is "triple the number of GPs" you are at least going to have to go back and check that. And perhaps find another answer.

You are also going to have to consider the impact of time on your plans before you work out whether it is appropriate or not. Quite a lot can happen over time: Demand can change, up or down. Trainees can become available. Staff can retire (this is difficult to assess these days, but it should still be estimated). Finally, turnover figures will tell us about likely leavers.

Step Four: Align Output to Challenge

If you have ended up with multiple options, a great way of choosing the best one is by aligning the options back to the challenge. This is something that really should be done all the time throughout the redesign, to stop us going too far down an inappropriate route.

Even with only one option, you need to make sure that it meets the challenge. If not, then you haven't met the brief, and you may need to go back round the redesign again. Although this time, you may want to bring the sponsor along with you to explain the challenge again.

I say "may have to", because if the redesign you have developed makes sense, and has support from the team, then it may be worth checking with the sponsor to see if it is good enough. They may be able to slightly adjust the challenge, if the redesign is compelling.

Step Five: Appraise Options

Once you've done all of this great work, you will end up with some options. One option is always the "do-nothing", which isn't the current state, it's what would happen if there was no transformation (current plus any likely changes to demand and staffing). You may have a plethora of other options though for all sorts of reasons. You may not have complete agreement between the parties for a start (no-one can force people to agree) so you might want to reflect a couple of choices. The agreed choice, even if you have one, might not actually meet the exam question.

So you might end up with a few options:

- Do nothing.
- Various options with different levels of stakeholder buy-in. This is normally based around a core (which is agreed), with some tweaks.
- An option without or with only minimal stakeholder buy-in, but that meets/better meets the challenge.

Each option can then be assessed as to the degree to which it is:

Safe: Generally a "yes" or "no" question.

Affordable: In terms of ongoing and implementation or one-off costs.

Of high enough quality or service-user experience?

Aligned with strategy and other programmes?

Agreed by the right stakeholders representing the front-line?

Implementable? For example are the required digital solutions available?

Amina and Fiona's view

When redesigning workforce, you need to be careful to create roles that work for real people - that's one of the main reasons for doing this with people, not to them. We are in "a war for talent" so super-efficient mechanical roles may not be wanted by anyone and could be bad for retention.

We don't get many chances at redesign, so its worth making sure that we do this one well.

Step Six: Validate and Refine Options

Once you've reached this stage, you need to re-engage with the steering group and agreed other stakeholders to validate and agree the right options. Working with this group, you need to ensure that it meets the requirements, and that everyone understands the value and cost of each option.

If the options fail to meet the requirements, then you may have to go back round the engagement or even data collecting stages again. Hopefully not, but I have had to re-do engagement before, engaging system leaders in the actual workshops so as to better align the expectations of the system leadership and those on the front line.

Once you have assessed the options, and agreed them with the steering group, they can be officially signed off for modelling, preferably with a few options to allow for greater engagement with stakeholders later in the process.

By the end of this step, you should have:

- A compelling current state picture to drive redesign.
- A future state, or set of future states describing the future process, organisation, workforce, digital tools etc.
- Options appraisal.

Now we need to assess the impact in a model…

Focus: Workforce Redesign Planning - The Seven R's

So, you've worked out your new model, and how many people you are going to need. Now you've got to consider how you are going to fill the gaps. Luckily, there is an easy way to think through what your plans need to be: The seven R's.

1. **Recruit:** Hire people, either internationally, nationally or locally.
2. **Retain:** Stop people leaving.
3. **Return:** Convince people who have left to return to work.
4. **Replace:** Replace the role through automation (RPA, AI etc), or different staff.
5. **Retrain:** Retrain other roles to do it.
6. **Redesign:** Redesign the role.
7. **Re-energise:** Reduce sickness and improve efficiency.

From this list, you can build a whole host of responses. You can train people, convince them to stay, recruit, make the place a great place to work, focus on wellness, introduce digital solutions and add in those new and enhanced roles that might need a whole host of actions on their own (new training programmes, recruitment, job descriptions etc).

So, let's consider ideas within each:

Recruit

This is an obvious one, and often the default. Assuming that demand is increasing, and with natural staff turnover, most workforce plans involve an increase in staff, and the simplest option is often to recruit more.

More nurses, more doctors, more GPs, more carers: Much of UK Health & Social Care workforce planning is about recruiting more of the same. Of course, this is now a major problem for a few reasons:

- COVID has increased global demand for healthcare professionals.
- Brexit has reduced the available number of staff to bring in from Europe.
- Demand has increased beyond national training numbers.

National bodies are trying to rectify the shortages, but this is no longer the easy option. Still, it does have a place, even now. Recruitment options for plans include:

- International recruitment efforts, which need to include international retention efforts (see later) if you are going to keep them long-term.

- National recruitment efforts, normally based around securing places for staff just out of training.

- Local "great place to live" efforts to bring people from other geographies.

- "National Health and Care Service is great" recruitment drives to bring people from other professions or private providers.

- School, college and university awareness schemes are longer-burn, but should form part of long-term plans.

- Analysis of where we aren't getting representation from the whole population, and drives to improve diversity in the recruitment process.

- Offering referral rewards.

- Offering "golden hellos".

- Covering the cost of tuition in return for joining (sponsorship).

- Increasing apprenticeships.

- Use of trainees as part of service delivery.

- Training people to do elements of their task early on, and then develop their expertise over time, rather than train everyone to be experts and then get them working.

A lot of this is competitive, so you can end up in bidding wars with others. Finding what people really want, and targeting individuals and groups is likely to be more effective than random engagement of multiple groups.

Retrain

Where we have a plentiful supply of available bodies, but with the wrong skills, can we re-train people to be able to take a useful role in the new process? This is a complex area with a few nuances due to it borrowing from the redesign element. Potential schemes are:

- Can we move tasks from areas where we have shortages to groups where we can more easily find staff? For example, can we move all calls from GPs to admin. staff. This can be called operating "at top of grade", but you have to be careful that you don't create work through hand offs, and jobs can get stressful if all of the easier tasks are taken away.

- Enhancing roles for existing clinicians, like Introducing Nurse Specialists etc.

- Get great unqualified staff to train to get qualified.

Return

I like this one, because it's not one you'd think of straight away, even though it used to be a staple of plans nationally. And it is one that we'll be revisiting a lot in the near future I think, as we search for inventive ways to increase the workforce. This area covers encouraging people to return to work in some way. Schemes include:

- Developing portfolio careers to get people to return.

- One-to-one planning for people that have left.

- National and regional "back to practice" schemes.
- Getting specialists to work on the ward for a day a week (look, I didn't say these were all good ideas, they are just ones I've seen).
- Creating options for people that have become disabled or ill to be able to return to work, or who have caring responsibilities.
- Post-retirement planning with individuals well in advance of retiring, to put in place a plan that could see at least some of their valuable skills and time retained in the service.

Retain

What can you do to stop people from leaving? This is all about reducing losses from your existing team, so is about focusing on those that you expect to leave in your future state. Assuming that physically preventing people from leaving isn't allowed, then you are left with a few options in this group:

- Holding proper appraisals regularly.
- Asking people what keeps people at work, and focusing on it.
- Effective reward structures, including appropriate financial reward, but also recognition, training and non-financial benefits.
- Holding effective leaver interviews, and developing plans to act on them.
- Developing portfolio careers to retain people longer, or job rotation to keep jobs interesting for longer.
- One-to-one planning for potential retirees to develop options for them to stay working.
- Electronically backed catalogue of attractive available roles.
- Analysis of retention rates, with action plans for low-retention areas and learning from high-retention areas.
- Communication and education of the value of caring work.
- Peer support and learning through structures like retention collaboratives.
- A focus on good leadership and good management at all levels.
- Organisation or system-wide monitoring and response to poor behaviour, like bullying etc.
- Access to mediation or discussion of work conflicts.

Re-energise

Re-energise is all about measures that aim to get more out of the people that are in the team already, either through doing more per person, or reducing absences from work. This can run from the punitive to the engaging, and includes:

- Targeted sickness level reduction schemes to include:
    - Monitoring;
    - Measuring; and
    - Undertaking, monitoring and acting on return to work interviews.

- Development and management of long-term sickness plans.
- Wellness being put at the heart of management (not just gym-memberships….).

Re-design

Redesign specifically covers a number of aspects including the definition of new roles and the streamlining of process:

- Introduction of new roles.
- Introducing expertise at the start of engagement.
- Combining roles to remove steps or duplication of effort.
- Reducing travel times.
- Introducing technology to reduce time: More efficient IT, computer systems that don't take half an hour to boot up. You know, advanced stuff.
- Introducing new equipment to reduce time, like digital dictation etc.
- Streamlining estate to make processes more efficient.
- Getting staff to work in different areas (e.g. mental health nurses in maternity) to combine support in one visit (and reduce demand).
- Use of multi-disciplinary teams.
- Streamlining organisations to reduce handoffs.
- Streamlining handoffs within organisations (especially at child to adult borders).

Replace

This is about finding ways to replace the need for some staff. In some ways you could call it "reduce" and still maintain the magical suite of "R"s that makes this section such a beautiful piece of classic literature. "Replace" covers reducing the amount of work that needs to be done or replacing workers with electronic or mechanical replacements. Think Skynet without the global destruction. Possible schemes include:

- Patient and service-user self-service or self-treatment
- Volunteer, carer and system-resilience efforts.
- Use of artificial intelligence.
- Use of robotic process automation to eliminate tasks that can be automated.

There you go, a big list of options to fill the gap.

Chapter 2.4

Modelling the Future State

Modelling is the fourth stage of this process, but in reality it's one that touches nearly every stage from mobilisation to implementation:

Mobilisation: At this point you tend to design your model and determine which type you are going to use.

At the ***current state*** stage, you need to collect the right data to populate your model.

In the ***future state*** stage you need to understand and document the assumptions that the group will use to determine what the future option(s) will look like. The model itself can be used to great effect in the workshops to either bring the current picture to life (CLEAR does this really well) or to model the future in front of the group.

In the ***modelling*** stage. I probably don't need to explain this one, as this chapter is all about it...

In ***implementation***, the model can be used to drive the business case, to model changes that occur and to leave behind as a mechanism for continuous improvement.

So modelling touches every step in the process, but for the sake of a beautiful linear narrative (which we need for a book like this – unless you want this to go all Cloud Atlas), we talk about modelling the future state following the workshop. Modelling the future state involves two steps:

Modelling the options in WRaPT, Excel or another tool. This in itself can be split into Design; Build; Test and Populate.

Validating the options to identify the way forward.

So let's start with the modelling:

Modelling the options

You may remember from our approach to developing individuals (the pyramid. Or tetrahedron) that alongside training we recommend providing tools and techniques to provide structure and a common language. These can then be used in a real project. Using appropriate tools is part of that, and can help embed the training in something concrete.

When we undertake modelling, we use two types of tools:

Existing, pre-made tools: These are generally the best kind, because they should be designed for the purpose, be safer for the use of personal data and be available after the initial redesign project ends. We typically use HEE's online WRaPT tool but have also engaged with others like Apex Insight and some pre-written and professionalised Excel models in the past.

The trouble with pre-made tools is that they may require you to learn some new skills (when you are already comfortable with your chosen generic tool), and they may only work in the way the developers intended, which means they sometimes can't do the little thing you wanted them to do. Sometimes they also cost money, so it is worth also being able to build your own in something generic.

Modelling on generic software: Usually Excel or Tableau, the development of bespoke models on a package like this has the advantage of being able to be designed specifically for the job you are doing.

In our experience, Excel models are prone to error and we used to regularly overestimate the level of skill in front line teams to use Excel and underestimate their ability to break models we've built. I once spent three hours trying to work out what was wrong with one model, only to find someone had "enhanced" it by adding formulas in white text. Yes, I'm talking to you Bernie.

We won't teach you how to build tools in any particular package so you'll have to develop your individual package skills through training, trial and error and practice. However, we'll discuss some wider points about building a workforce model, and talk you through it.

We'll consider this in two parts:

Basic Modelling

Basic modelling involves matching activity to workforce, which is why we talk about three basic pieces of data that you need (as we saw back in the data section):

Workforce: Broken down into each unique type (role, numbers, cost).

Activity: Broken down into types with numbers for each.

Drivers: The link between the two.

There are also some specific things that you will probably need to model:

What happens to the activity we can do if we reduce or increase the number of people we have in specific roles?

What would the impact be of greater or less efficiency?

If activity goes up, how many more people do we want?

What are the different costs of various options or scenarios?

You may also want to consider the cost impact of these changes and the differences between current, commissioned and budget levels.

Any model that you produce should be able to produce at least one scenario. That is to say that a model can start with the baseline, and then changes can be applied that result in a future state or scenario.

Thus, a simple model can be structured as:

- Current staffing and activity.
- Changes.
- Future staffing and activity.

The fun with that straight away is that you have to pick a constant, because there are two factors that can change. When you increase staff, activity increases. When you increase activity, staff needed

Amina and Fiona's view

Collecting drivers (the link between workforce and activity) is the job that takes the most time, as it generally requires talking to teams to understand who is doing what. We like to produce working examples as quickly as possible though, and it is possible to make assumptions as to who does what as a hypothesis, and then check this later with the team.

increases. When you increase efficiency you either need less staff or you can do more activity with the staff you have.

Typically, you should pick activity as the standard: Putting the service-user at the centre of your model is generally the right thing to do, so that whenever you model, you are modelling "How many people do I need to deliver the activity?", not "how much activity can my team do?" It's up to you which one you pick, or you can build complexity into your model to allow you to choose (as WRaPT does).

So, a simple model should have at least one scenario or option, but it is always better to be able to present multiple options as we discussed earlier. So, your model should be able to produce:

- Current staffing and activity.
- Option 1 (No change).
  - Changes (due to time etc).
  - Future staffing and activity.
- Other options (multiple).
  - Changes (due to redesign).
  - Future staffing and activity.

More Advanced Modelling

The above, simple, modelling is actually far from simple once you move beyond a single team. If you are doing this for a whole system, to build a baseline, then you are talking about the need to share models with your line manager, aggregate models, build in new roles, calculate the impact of changes across hundreds of teams etc. And then you start needing to use a bespoke tool like WRaPT, which can do all of the above.

However, advanced modelling can be more than just going bigger. There are lots of other things that you might want to model.

Activity: This is the big one, and one that I often use Excel for, before using WRaPT. The CLEAR approach uses its bespoke models to create Sankey diagrams showing the flow of activity, and interactive models showing the underlying source of the referral, and attaching complexity or condition to the patient as they come into Emergency Departments. That sort of data is (a) incredibly engaging for clinicians and allows for evidence-based redesign and (b) actually isn't needed for the workforce modelling. You can do that analysis in Excel or Tableau, and then model the impact in WRaPT or your own model.

It is, however, incredibly useful to be able to play with activity before you even get to workforce, so it is well worth ensuring that any model you build allows for this sort of analysis.

Factors such as age to identify likely retirees: If you are specifically looking at this as a topic, then your model may need to be able to reflect this, but in general I avoid it like the proverbial plague. The holding of protected characteristics (in this case, year of birth and gender), means upping your Information Governance game, and makes most generic tools inappropriate. Second, you are making big assumptions about retiring, when we don't have a lot of information on when people will retire just based on age and gender, given recent changes.

Finally, if you are modelling a small team

you'll probably know the individuals and thus can model based on knowledge, or it will be a big team and you can just use national figures to estimate the impact.

Modelling different factors (e.g. travel times for care visits, single-occupancy wards): Oh, this is a good one. You really know what you are talking about asking that question.

The great thing about inpatient settings, community teams, primary care operations of most sorts etc, is that you can build a model once and apply it across multiple wards, teams or practices. You work out what they do, how long it takes etc, multiply it by activity and hey presto you can say "that practice needs three GPs, four nurses, three receptionists and a pharmacist".

Great. And then the Practice Manager, who is struggling to cope with current staff numbers already twice that, comes along and kicks you somewhere sensitive. And quite rightly. Because every practice is different, and you need to take account of that. We'll look at this in a bit under the multi-site model.

Can we overlay some different benchmarks of efficiency?: Sometimes, you want to play with overlaying efficiency levels from different sources. What if we applied a top 25% efficiency to this? What if we applied the best of a group? That requires that you have a table of benchmarks that a model can choose from.

Personally, I believe that all benchmarks are evil, so it's not something I tend to worry about. This can generally be done by agreeing the assumptions we are going to use and then applying them, but if you want this sort of functionality then a more complex model is needed. Older versions of WRaPT could do this, but as it was unused, they were not continued in later versions.

What is the impact of safer staffing levels?: One thing that requires much more advanced techniques is the application of safer staffing levels or some sort of "base" figure. I remember from my retail days, some card shops would have no customers at all in on some days, and some hours of the day but yet staff are needed in store (you can't just leave the whole place empty).

Of course, people can do various other tasks (tidy up, put out new stock, do the banking etc) but eventually, you run out of jobs to do. So you need to apply a "if there is no work then you need people in anyway" rule, and then you are into more advanced analytics. Even more advanced is playing in the impact of shift patterns (you can't ask people to come in for one hour at a time just because you have a massive spike in customers as they have to be there for a decent shift (say, four hours). In an annual model, like most workforce models, this is something that requires a different set of data (hourly information), so I would do analysis like this outside my workforce model and then apply the learning in my assumptions.

Types of model

There are three main types of model that I work with: Percentage; Bottom up activity; and Multi-team

Percentage model: I've mentioned before that there are a couple of ways you can model workforce. The first way is using the percentage approach. The way this works is that you work out how much of each person's time is spent on various activities and their fixed tasks. Thus, you have may have ten nurses, who spend 50% of their time delivering inpatient activity (3,000 bed nights per year) and 50% of their time delivering outpatient clinics (1,000 new appointments per year).

The advantage of this is that it is real. Those people do spend that amount of time and get through that much activity. It takes into account all the other tasks and downtime that don't link to actual activity, and lumps it into the activity time. This makes things very simple and allows you to separate this if you wish into a "fixed" time. There is little chance of getting it badly wrong, as long as you do count all the activity and all the staff that delivered it. To do that you need to ensure that bank, agency and overtime is included.

Bottom-up activity: The second way to do it is to add up what everyone does. Thus you work out that delivering activity A takes sixty minutes, and that the team does 10,000 per year. You can work out that you need 600,000 minutes of staff time to deliver it. You can go further and break it down into its constituent parts: Five minutes of filing, twenty minutes of preparation, thirty minutes of care provision and five minutes of admin.

Amina and Fiona's view

When we design models in WRaPT, we normally use high-level activity information to simplify the modelling a bit. For example, if you can use new outpatient referrals as the one activity to model, that is easier than having new appointments, follow up appointments, letter pages typed, letters printed, discharges made etc. But if you need to go to that level then do it - and WRaPT can do that too!

You are also able to model things that affect efficiency like DNA (Did Not Attend) rates and sickness rates.

The bottom-up activity approach is great when you know what you are doing, because you are able to be very specific about all the different things that make up the role, and that allows for more specific redesign. You can build a model that multiplies all the activity by all the times they take and get to a bottom-up view on how long everything takes.

The trouble is, it doesn't. What about holidays, training and bank holidays? They are easy enough to work out and add, and in fact this is normally taken into account in medical planning (activity delivered over 40-44 weeks) and in nursing (the 23 to 27% that is added to establishments).

But then what about all the other things, the stuff that we sometimes call "downtime"? Breaks, the time it takes to move between tasks, to re-do tasks you've done wrong, the time to deal with the unexpected etc. You can't easily work that out, yet it can be 30% of the time. At one point I practically had a full-time job following a well-known consultancy around, correcting staffing models that failed to take into account downtime appropriately.

Even if you take account of downtime, you can build a model that doesn't add up to the number of people that have delivered the activity across the year. If I've learned one thing, it is that you can't just go "oh well, now I'll assume that everyone can work to the timings and I've already made a saving". It doesn't go down well if you just tell people they can do more activity with what they've got. You have to help them discover and understand what changes they can make in order to be able to deliver activity differently (and hopefully more efficiently). Thus, it is important to work out, or help the team work out, why there is a difference between their staff numbers and their calculated numbers.

Multi-team: A multi-team model is a version of the bottom-up activity model, in which you develop a standard model which is then applied to all similar teams: Wards, community teams, retailers shops etc. Using this approach you can develop a model for wards that could potentially be used for each one in each hospital in the country.

To do this, you need to add an element that takes into account the differences that each ward legitimately has. Again, back in retail days, there were all sorts of things that made a difference, like:

- Distance to stockroom, has an impact on re-stocking.
- Multiple floors, has an impact on security.
- Different items can take longer to sell than others, so you need to take into account what is sold, not just how many in total.
- Customers can come in different patterns due to things like distance to bus stations.
- Time in service can change how many holidays people get.
- Number of part-time staff can sometimes be less efficient (sometimes more) because they all need to do some fixed stuff.
- Applying a standard percentage for maternity leave doesn't make sense, so you need to take into account actual maternity rates. I would say the same for sickness rates (although there is a school of thought that applying a standard rate rewards teams for low sickness rates, thus keeping sickness low. Yes, I know it doesn't work....).

As mentioned earlier, when building a multi-site model, and applying these variables differently across an estate you are going to end up with some that are above the current staff levels and others below. You can't just give people more hours randomly, without working out why they are more efficient than the model. And you can't just cut hours without finding out why they are so much less efficient. You need to investigate, amend and explain what changes are needed. Maybe they take twice as long over some things and need some training?

Building a Model: The Steps

There are five sub steps for building a model. This book doesn't aim to cover the detail of modelling, which is a whole set of skills in itself, but it may be useful to understand the basics:

Design happens at the start, although the way it works will likely be adapted

Amina and Fiona's view

We describe the building the model approach here in five steps, but if you are using WRaPT you follow the two steps of the WRaPT: Redesign approach. WRaPT has already been designed and tested. So all you need to do is to create the model scenarios in WRaPT and then validate these with the project steering group and stakeholders.

throughout the various parts of the programme if it is allowed. Designing the model carefully requires an understanding of:

- Data that you are expecting to use.
- Outcomes that you require.
- Analysis needed to drive change.

Building a model is a specialised skill in itself. Things worth considering include:

- Using different colours for input, calculation and output cells.
- Protecting cells that are not used for entry to avoid the risk of people making mistakes or breaking the spreadsheet.
- Ensuring that entry cells will only allow the correct format.
- Annotating all aspects of the model to aid people in testing and interpreting results.
- Consider whether it is best to use complex calculations that are difficult to audit, or building up the calculations across multiple cells, which can create more possibilities for error. In general, annotated complex calculations tend to work best, but either approach can work.

Testing a model is vital. Errors can occur even in the bespoke packages, so light checking of outputs is sensible even with them. With the generic packages, like Excel, errors are far more likely and therefore a testing regime is needed. We normally consider:

- Self-testing during which you document expected and actual results.
- Peer-testing, which should be documented again.
- User-testing - and you guessed it, documented again.

Populate the model using available data – this is usually really quick once you've actually collected the right stuff.

Validate the outputs with the stakeholders, checking that it makes sense, and then taking them through a process so that they really consider what is coming out.

Developing models is, as we said, a specialist skill in its own right, but everyone should be able to learn the basics of tools like WRaPT and Excel in order to create simple models. They aren't as scary as they seem!

By the end of this step, you should have:

- A workforce model (either built and populated), or a populated WRaPT model.
- Modelled options.
- Documented test results.

Focus: The Importance of Equality, Diversity and Inclusion

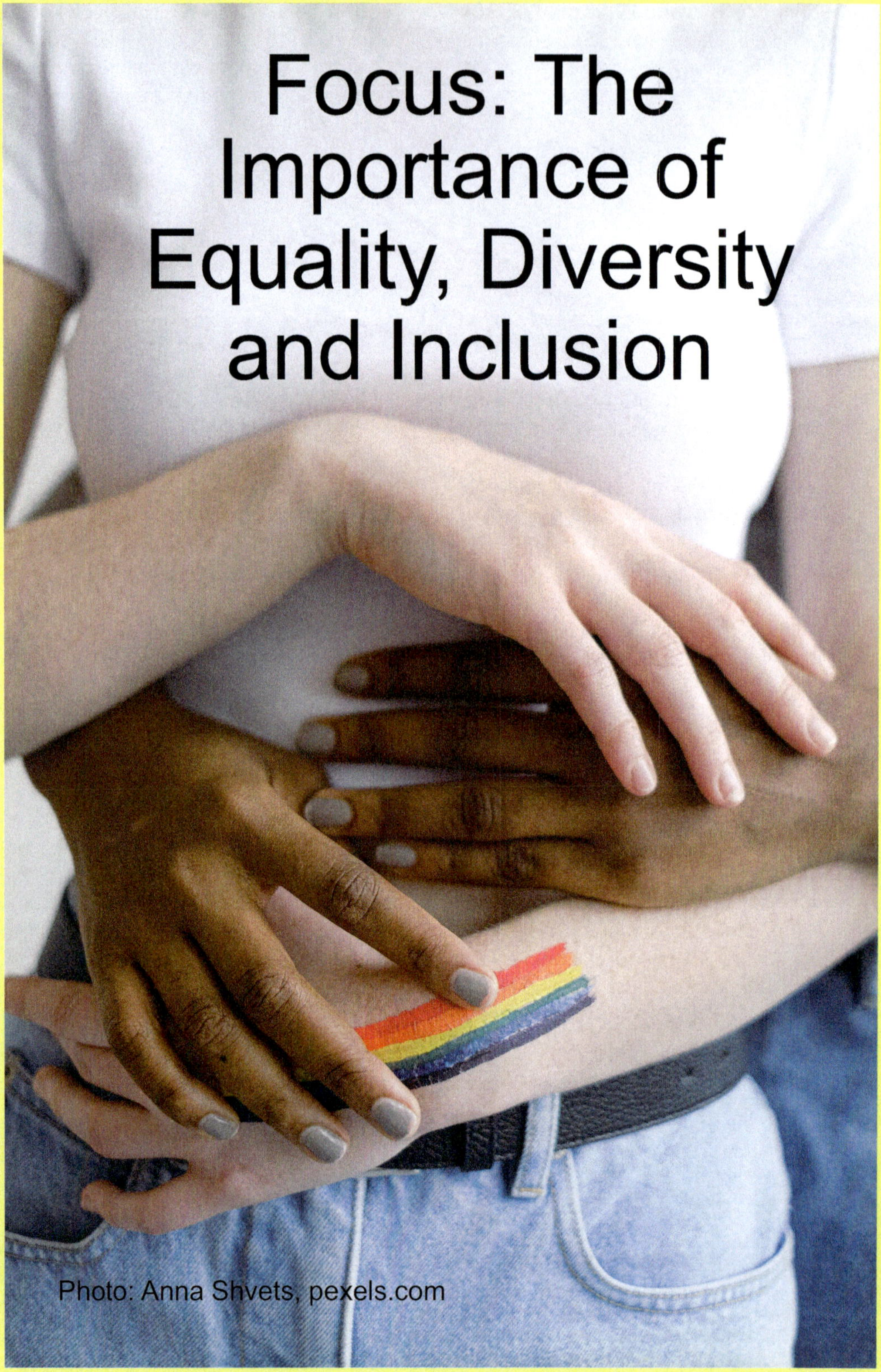

Photo: Anna Shvets, pexels.com

The Equality Act 2010 outlines the different aspects of equality: Age, disability, gender reassignment, marital status, pregnancy, motherhood, race, religion, belief, sex and sexual orientation. Equality, Diversity and Inclusion (EDI) is all about making sure that everyone is included and we work to build equality. And before we start with it, we need to accept that it isn't always easy.

Getting a representative cross section is just not going to happen every time, but just like all the other barriers to workforce planning, it's worth doing everything you can. But why? For a start, it's the right thing to do. But if you need more than that, there are three main reasons:

- ***Service-users:*** Outcomes will be better if we build processes around the diverse needs of the population.

- ***Workforce:*** We are in a fight for workforce. wW need to be attractive to 100% of the population and we want those people to be happy.

- ***Communities:*** These need to be able to draw on the assets of a wide group. Only if diverse groups understand each other will this happen.

We need to consider all aspects of EDI in workforce planning:

- When undertaking workforce redesign we need to bring in a diverse set of views, so need to engage a diverse set of workforce. Can you bring diversity to your programme team, or engage diverse speakers in future state events?

- We must reflect diversity as part of patient engagement.

- We need to use appropriate metrics to understand the diversity of service-users and workforce and whether recruitment etc, is working equally for these groups.

- When a change is agreed, an impact assessment will help you work through whether the change is inclusive.

- Why not get expert advice from an EDI professional when you are undertaking your redesign?

In summary, equality, diversity and inclusion is important and needs effort, so let's take a mindful approach to this.

Chapter 2.5

Implementing the Change

Not all approaches have an implementation section, but what's the point in redesigning everything if you don't actually implement the changes?

Implementation, as a stage, is as important as all the others. It pulls heavily on project management skills, like stage one does, and includes four steps:

- ***Documenting the case*** to set out the benefits and costs.
- ***Planning actions.***
- ***Planning benefits realisation*** processes to monitor and adjust and make sure that the challenge is met.
- ***Leading the change.***.

The approach we take to implementation is based on project management but also pulls heavily on Kotter's change model.

This model, from his 1995 book, "Leading Change" sets out eight steps for change, which all need to be done well to succeed in a change initiative. His steps are:

- Creating a sense of urgency.
- Forming a guiding coalition.
- Creating a vision for change.
- Communicating the vision.
- Removing obstacles.
- Creating short term wins.
- Building on the change.
- Anchoring the change within the organisation's culture.

By considering the mechanics of project management and the steps in Kotter's model we can give ourselves a great chance of actually implementing the change that we have designed. We will consider each of these eight steps as we go through the steps of WRaPT: Redesign. This is all a bit confusing because we have two sets of steps, so I'll refer to Kotter's as principles as we go through.

So let's have a look at the WRaPT: Redesign steps:

Documenting the Case

This bit sounds a bit dull and process-focused, but it isn't. This is your chance to communicate the change, to engage that powerful coalition through established routes for investment and prioritisation within organisations.

The point of this is to secure the investment that you need in time and money through communicating the project, its benefits and the consequences for not doing it. It is not about who can write the biggest document; this is a time for communication and careful thought.

I see this stage as a sale. It's a transaction, certainly as you want something (funding, support, agreement) and the people making the decision will be getting something. So you can approach this whole process in a couple of ways. One way is to see it like selling something simple, like a bag of crisps. The customer will buy the crisps if they want crisps. It's there, and it's up to them whether they buy it or not.

The way I prefer to look at it is like selling something new and expensive in a competitive environment. They don't know if they need it, they have other things vying for their attention and money, and they need to get the agreement of others in order to buy it.

So, you need to sell it to them, and to their colleagues. What makes business cases exciting is that they are a combination of vision, plan and sales document.

A well-written business case can take many forms, because: The projects will be different sizes and types; you need to operate within the processes of your organisation or system; and you must consider the needs of the stakeholders in the process.

So, the first step is to find out what the investment process is in your organisation and who the key stakeholders are (especially those who make the decision).

Before we get into what I think they should include, the most important thing is to find out what the stakeholders want. They might just need a small board paper that they can use along with a presentation, to secure funding and agree resources. They may need you to go through their Business or Capital Planning processes. They may need a full five-case model to be presented through multiple gateways to secure agreement nationally. I've personally been involved in all three of these types within the health sector in the UK.

However, finding out what format people need is certainly not the end of the engagement. You are looking to get your work funded and supported, and to build that powerful coalition. So, you need to continually engage with the key stakeholders in order to:

- ***Build in their expertise:*** Senior leaders have a lot of experience in what makes a good business case. Engaging these leaders throughout the process of building the case will improve its quality.
- ***Gain buy-in:*** By engaging these leaders, they feel much more involved, and are more likely to understand it, and (very importantly) green-light it.
- ***Help them pitch it:*** If you hand a business case to someone and walk away, you no longer have any influence on when it gets considered, how it is sold and how much support it gets. Maintaining contact (and polite pressure) to make sure it is submitted to the right groups in the right way, quickly, as well as offering to present the case yourself (with supporting information from service-users and clinicians) will give the case a better chance of success.
- **Educate and influence the decision makers and the influencers:** This complex sale will probably need to engage more than one person, and each one of them will have a range of people they rely on for their views. So, we need to

Amina and Fiona's view

Because WRaPT was funded by HEE, we have had to prove value for money in its use. It is not acceptable to just have a good redesign that everybody likes; it has to be implemented. The approach we take is to develop a case study, which needs an understanding of the benefits expected and of those achieved. We go back to teams we have worked with to check on how they have done, and to write up their success. Why not do the same for your project?

identify who the buyers and their influencers are, develop an engagement plan for each and implement it. If we really want to go to town we can also identify who the competitors are, and develop a plan to augment our case to beat those other cases. But we might now be going too far…

There are a couple of models for business cases that we will talk about in a little bit, but for me there are some key elements that you need to consider even in an informal single page case:

Every case should include a couple of summaries: President Schwarzenegger in The Simpsons Movie, randomly chooses an option when faced with a decision, saying "I was elected to lead, not to read", which sums up many busy hospital executives I've met in my time. They are busy people, so you need to grab their attention quickly. Plus, as Einstein said, if you can't describe something simply you don't understand it. You don't see quotes from Einstein and The Simpsons in one paragraph very often…

A good case should include:

- A paragraph-long "elevator pitch": Named because you should be able to describe this to someone (generally an important person) in the time it takes to travel in a lift.

- A half or one-page summary.

A compelling vision: This is one of the Kotter elements. Each case should include a compelling vision for the future.

Options: A good business case should include a range of options (including a "do nothing" view). This allows people to buy into solutions even if things change before it is approved. It also allows some control over the process for people, which makes it more palatable to agree.

Clear benefits and costs for each option: The case needs to have clear benefits, preferably quantifiable and hard metrics that hit the requirements of the stakeholders. The costs need to be reasonable, and similarly clear.

Patients, team members and clinicians: In order to build the options you've certainly engaged all of these groups, and you need to build on this for the case. These groups, especially patients and clinicians, can have a somewhat talismanic impact on people making the decisions. People are unique, and what influences them is unique to them, but in my experience, getting the voices of patients and clinicians into the case (either the document, or as presenters) is always a good idea.

There are a couple of business case models that are worth taking account of:

The Three-Phase Model

The Three-Phase model is an HM Treasury Model, that gets used a lot in UK Healthcare both in secondary care and in health and care systems. In healthcare it has been adapted to add a fourth phase in some hospitals I have worked at. A bit like Project Management methods, this can be applied lightly, or incredibly formally, depending on the requirements of the project. To be honest, In complex environments, I'd call in professional help once you get beyond the Strategic Outline Case.

Concept paper: An initial high-level view of the change, the issues it is addressing and the expected benefits. This should be enough to engage people in building the case up into the more formal stages, and is normally done before the project even really starts in earnest. By getting a view in early, it can help build up engagement from senior leaders.

Strategic outline case (SOC): The aim of this stage is to assess the strategic fit. This stage includes the strategic context, service need (current issues etc), options, benefits/affordability, milestones and deliverability assessments.

Outline business case (OBC): This builds on the SOC and becomes much more complex by adding a detailed appraisal of options, highlighting a best value for money option, preparing for procurement, confirming funding and affordability and setting out an outline plan for delivery.

Full business case (FBC): This is where it gets even more complex. An FBC is a final, technical document normally undertaken after the outcome of the procurement process. It includes a detailed delivery plan and contractual arrangements.

The Five-Case model

The Five-Case model is another HM Treasury approach and can be used with the three-phase model. It sets out five "cases" or areas that need to be considered to build a full case. The five cases are:

Strategic: Is there a strategic fit and a clear case for change? This part considers the change reasons.

Economic: Is this the best balance of benefits, cost and deliverability? This part of the model considers the financial reason for the change.

Commercial: This section considers who will deliver this, and the best commercial deal.

Financial: This considers where we will secure the funding and whether we can influence the costs.

Management: This section sets out how we will deliver the project, including governance.

So, to sum up, we need to engage the stakeholders, develop and write the case and then engage the stakeholders again in discussing and agreeing the case.

Planning Actions

Like all of these, implementation isn't really a linear process. Whilst you are going through the Business Planning step you will need to develop an increasingly detailed set of delivery plans and view on the delivery process through new governance.

If you haven't done it already, this is the point where you may need to go back to your seven R's to actually plan how you intend to move from needing thirty more care workers to a reality when you actually have those people, they are meeting the needs of the service and that they are suitably embedded so that they are getting the best experience (and not intending to immediately leave).

In reality, the implementation stage is really a handoff from the design stage, which will mean several things that you developed in the mobilisation stage need to be reconsidered. We will go through each of these next:

Amina and Fiona's view

Looking back to Kotter's model, we can see that the business case has a significant role in creating and communicating the vision for change, and also in forming the powerful coalition that we will need.

So it is worth getting it right for the sake of the change, as well as to generate investment.

New Governance

The governance for the redesign has done us proud up until now, but we may now need a new team and approach if we are to deliver the project. We will need to determine this, document it for the case and put it into place if the case is agreed. The business case will include this information (mainly in the management case element if following that approach).

Steering group: Do we need a new Chair (and deputy), administration, agenda and objectives for the group? Almost certainly we will need to change who it reports to and how. This can all be captured in a new terms of reference. Kotter's model requires that we remove obstacles to delivery, so we need an engaged and effective steering group to do that. They are also part of that powerful coalition for change.

Project Manager and team: Delivery of the programme may require new resources, including project management, new advisors and delivery team. The costs of these will need to be established, which should include those of the direct team as well as a view on the costs of staff involved in the change (including double-running costs). Anything that is not the new "business as usual" should be considered in the costs.

Monitoring: If we've identified the resources that will deliver the project, we now need to develop the mechanisms for monitoring progress and success. This includes:

- ***Benefits breakdown:*** We'll talk about the benefits realisation plan in a bit, but a key part of the governance needs to focus on monitoring the delivery of these benefits.
- ***Project milestone reports:*** The group will need to be able to monitor, manage and adjust delivery of the project against planned milestones.
- ***Other indicators:*** All the other things you need to monitor as you go through implementation including risks and various quality indicators.

New Plan

If you are going to monitor progress against plan, you are going to need a plan, and unless you had some next-level skills and foresight at the start of the project, you are going to need a new one for the implementation. As you can see from the business case section, a plan can be little more than a set of key milestones, an outline set of actions or a fully detailed set.

In reality, most plans fit somewhere around the middle with enough detail to be able to see what is being done, highlight the key milestones and be able to monitor progress. Too much, and the message gets hidden amongst the detail of who is going to do what detailed action on which site, too little and is difficult to spot whether the programme is falling behind or not.

Again, referencing Kotter, the plan should include some short term wins – this helps build the legend of success for the project, as well as making sure that we get value for the time that people have already put into the project.

New Engagement and new Communication Plan

The stakeholders in many cases will be broadly the same, but the way you impact them (and thus how they may impact you) will change. You may have redesigned the workforce with a small number of patients, but now all patients will be affected. The same will be true of the front line-staff and other stakeholders. You should have identified the best representatives, and they should have been clearly communicating throughout to their constituencies, but the reality is that life rarely goes to plan, and you will need to reconsider your engagement and communication strategy from scratch.

It's probably a good time to introduce the wisdom of one of my previous bosses, who's view was that people need to be able to answer three questions before accepting change:

Why change? As with Kotter's model, people need to know what the point of changing is.

What is in it for me? They need to know what it specifically improves for them.

How will I cope? As a final thought, people need to be able to work through how they will personally deal with the changes that directly affect them. They will be worried about a range of things: Workload, personal relationships, status etc.

Amina and Fiona's view

Refreshing everything at this stage is a cathartic thing to do. In many cases, the redesign project mobilisation was sub-par, so the implementation project is a chance to get it right. The mobilisation session for the implementation can celebrate the success of the redesign, plan the success of this next phase and allow for a proper handover to new people. You can also plan when you will come back to check on implementation progress!

Also when dealing with teams, it is worth considering the impact of individual stakeholders on the group, and whether that is a communication issue or something else. Traditional project approaches give us a three or five level view of individuals. In one model individuals are tagged as Blockers, Followers or Supporters (generally on a bell curve showing that most people are followers).

Other models expand this a little by having Advocates at one end and Opponents at the other. In the middle you get Followers, Indifferent (these people make up the bulk of the bell curve) and Blockers.

I like this expanded view, because it introduces a real distinction that the shorter model does not. In the expanded model you have opponents who will lose something through the change, and no matter what you do you are not going to shift their thinking. In more complex projects, I come across these people quite often.

Now, this is a scale, and no named group behaves exactly the same. As you move from Opponents to Blockers, some of these people might still have a perceived issue, but they can be won round with more information. Some of these people are just going to be difficult, and whilst you need to be aware of their impact on others, appeasing these people takes Chamberlain-level concessions, and will be about as successful.

As you move more into the Blockers, the challenge is to educate, and work on the three questions (Why change? What is in it for me? How will I cope?).

On the other side you have the Advocates who are generally those that are already gaining from the project and need little engagement, into the followers who are generally well intentioned towards the project.

Many of this group, plus the indifferent ones, are the ones worth focusing your effort on. If this is a bell curve, note how many people will fall into the Indifferent group, and it is this large group that needs to have regular communication. Otherwise you are risking a sizeable majority deciding not to engage with the solution through a lack of information (or misinformation from those that are opponents). Kotter highlighted the need to build a volunteer army, and this group is a great one to recruit.

The reason to do this stakeholder analysis is to identify how (and when, who etc) you are going to engage with groups and individuals. That needs to be the outcome from this mental model.

So, three big lessons from me:

1. Some people are just going to be against the project, and it is not worth trying to convince them.

2. You need to engage with the silent majority to bring them on board.

3. Never write the base analysis down. This is a mental model for dealing with groups, not a spreadsheet or whiteboard tool for assigning labels to people.

Great. So now you have a new plan, new governance and new engagement approaches. Just a couple more things to consider before we complete the business case and deliver the change.

Planning Benefits Realisation

Kotter's model requires that we build on the change and anchor it within the organisation's culture. The business case requires that we have a clear benefits case and a plan for realising it.

Just as the planning step, above, represents a handover from the design to the implementation, during implementation you get a handover to business as usual. You cannot declare "Mission Accomplished" on the implementation until the new model is working within the day-to-day operations of the business.

In the implementation stage, a great start is the development of a business realisation plan. You are really trying to make sure that everyone can see how this project fits in the delivery of agreed organisation strategy, and helping the project see what is important to "the business" (generally senior management).

A benefits realisation plan includes:

An overview of the organisation's strategy: Of course, in the current health and social care environment, strategy is quite fluid, so you may need to engage with senior leaders to establish what the real strategy is, and this may include some pretty short-term elements as central and regional priorities shift.

Identification of how this programme will assist the strategy: Highlighting exactly how much of the strategy the programme will address, preferably quantitative, but qualitative data is also useful.

Breakdown of expected benefits, including:

- ***Description:*** Description of the benefit.
- ***Value:*** Quantification of the benefit.
- ***Timescale:*** Expected date of benefit realisation.
- ***Benefits owner:*** Who is responsible for delivering them.
- ***Benefitting group:*** Who will benefit from the change and sign it off at the end.
- ***Plan:*** Linked to the overall plan, detailed steps or milestones for delivery of the benefits.

This stuff sounds heavy, and in reality you often don't get to this stage in a programme. But it is very important to engage the business in how they will operationalise the new workforce. There are examples of new roles not being integrated properly into operations, and the benefits not being realised. Only by chasing the benefits can we be sure that all has been implemented.

Leading the Change

Up until now, we've covered some quite managerial elements like building plans and governance structures. All of these will make a difference, but they are not enough on their own. The final element, and the thing that binds all of this together is the leadership of the delivery of the change.

Leadership is one of the most defined, yet most undefinable parts of your job. The reality is that a set of your skills, experiences, attitudes, beliefs and behaviours, when combined with those of others in your team will interact with those of a complex set of stakeholders, hopefully successfully.

Kotter's model for leading change, sets out the eight steps required for change to be successful. Whilst it is a model for leading change, many of its aspects have already been covered in the sections above. However, there are some key leadership considerations that are worth considering:

Creating a sense of urgency: More than ever, the health and care system across the country requires bold change.

Amina and Fiona's view

As we highlighted earlier, we need to evaluate our impact on each project. So a further step that could be added after implementation is "Evaluation". It is definitely one to think about: What are your actions going to be to check how well this has gone? Could we get more benefit by a quick refresh after six months? Should we introduce some form of Continuous Improvement?

Quickly. Yet, as we learned all the way back at the start of this unnecessarily long book, workforce planning is impossible. Leadership is needed to break through this deadlock, and create a sense of urgency.

Forming a guiding coalition: Dealing with the impossible will only be possible if leaders across health and care work together, possibly to the financial detriment of their own organisations. This will only be done if you can form a powerful guiding coalition so you need to be able to engage leaders across multiple organisations and lead them to support the change.

Creating and communicating a vision for change: Communication plans are all very well, but communication is a fluid, human thing. You should be able to lead your team to develop effective and real communication, and your own leadership communication skills will be needed if you are to sell a compelling vision.

Removing obstacles: Raising delays to projects is easy, as is forgiving people for not doing their bit for the change: They are busy, you understand that. It's an important part of leadership to remove the obstacles to delivery, and to keep busy teams on track.

Amina and Fiona's view

Getting the right skills and team together to deliver the programme of work is key. We have trained many people in workforce redesign, but it is not always about numbers trained. If the project hasn't been set up in the correct way and there is no Executive support / senior decision making and Clinical input then no matter how many you train, the project will struggle to make progress in its implementation.

By the end of this step, you should have:

- A documented business case.
- A benefits realisation plan.
- A project plan for implementation, including communication plan.
- New project governance arrangements in place.

WRaPT: Redesign Conclusion

In this section we have learned about WRaPT: Redesign, an approach to Workforce Redesign that also takes into account the need to change process, equipment, estates, digital tools and organisation structures to support the change. Whilst we have covered a considerable amount, we have only touched upon many of the skills needed and barely mentioned others. Process mapping, role redesign, change management, project management, facilitation, communications, business case development, planning, time management, leadership, resilience and in extreme cases, karate, are all skills that you may need as part of this journey. These are all skills for which a huge and growing body of development work is available on-line, so please continue your development journey there, on the Carados Ltd YouTube channel, on the HEE website or with the WRaPT team.

Hopefully by taking account of this lot, you've been able to implement a newly designed workforce. You've finished a non-linear process that started right back with scoping and mobilising the project. You've worked through understanding the current state and developing and modelling the future state. Finally, you've delivered the change.

Well done, because if you've managed to do all of this well, you've done better than I have. And if you have actually transformed workforce across health and social care, you have done the impossible. Well done indeed.

There's more to do though. The remaining sections of this book set out more approaches to elements of Workforce Planning, starting with developing the workforce plan.

SECTION THREE

DEVELOPING THE WORKFORCE PLAN OR STRATEGY

One thing you may well need to do is to write a workforce plan document. Writing a workforce plan or strategy document can be a pretty big undertaking for you and for others, so you need to make sure that it does its job.

You might think that transforming workforce on the ground to actually make a difference is the most important part of workforce planning. Well, if you do, then I don't agree. I think that developing the right workforce plan or strategy, and then driving it through, is the single best mechanism for getting everyone to pull in the same direction, to align workforce with other parts of the transformation and, crucially, for getting the money to make changes a reality. Your beautiful redesign will wither and die without the oxygen of money and attention, and the workforce strategy and plan is the way to get it.

The difference between a workforce strategy and a workforce plan is not entirely clear, as there is considerable overlap between them. If you are asked to develop one, you need to understand what they are for, and what is needed, and you may end up doing both.

Strategy: Generally shorter than the workforce plan, the strategy sets out the high level view. The strategy's aim is to set the agenda and communicate it, so that everything that happens aids towards its delivery. Of course, sometimes people call this a workforce plan, because we're not great at agreeing definitions in the world of workforce planning...

Plan: This is a larger, more detailed version of the strategy, its aim is to provide the detail on the case for change and plan and engage people in that detail. The strategy really summarises everything, whereas this document includes the detailed information. Some people define a workforce plan as the detailed workforce numbers, and indeed these can be included.

No matter what we call them, or how we split them, the approach to building them is the same. Apart from one word: Detail...

A Successful Plan

One of the phrases I use all the time is, "We need more teeth". This comes from Gray Mitchell, a character in the film Jurassic World. At one point there is a battle between a large, somewhat unhinged dinosaur, and some smaller more heroic dinosaurs (who are on the side of the goodies). At this exciting but unlikely point, one of the characters, Gray, summarises the solution by saying, "We need more teeth".

This then prompts another character to release a T-Rex to help out. Even against the backdrop of some really horrible decisions that she has made throughout the film, this seems like a bad idea, but it works. She also manages to outrun it in high heels. She's the one with the high heels, not the dinosaur.

Look, I know, I've gone into that in far too much detail on dinosaurs, but my point is that Gray was right. Whenever you want to do anything you need more teeth: More people on your side, more money to implement it, more focus on delivering this problem. You need more teeth.

The way you get these teeth is to make a compelling case, and work to secure leadership time and funding for the implementation. A great way to do that is to understand right at the start what is needed from the project. You need to consider:

How fast is the change needed? There is little point delivering a change in five years' time if we'll be swamped by demand in 6 months.

How big does it need to be? Is it just a tweak, or do we need transformation?

What is the financial saving needed? There is no point if it isn't going to meet the needs. I remember one programme where we were asked to save £40 million across eight workstreams, and one came back with a suggestion to model a team of only a few people. By knowing the scale needed, you can push back on expectations.

Where can investment come from? When is that investment available and what do we need to do to get it? This is vital as you need to know how to secure it, and when the money is coming available. A compelling and beautiful case in July may have missed the boat, when people were hunting around for schemes to spend their underspends on in February.

Is it possible? Hopefully this was covered in your SMART goals, but there really is no point talking about international recruitment if it is just not possible.

Focus: Whether it is for a case or for an implementation plan, we have found that it pays to find three big things to focus on (as per the excellent Minto approach). It's so much easier to sell and implement a change that has a simple vision based around three big things, than a 100-page, 5000-line change programme.

What is a Workforce Plan?

We'll go into the detail of the sections later on, but at its heart a workforce plan is a document that sets out the detail of how we plan to move from our current position, to a better future position. In order to do that it describes our current position and our future position, and generally has some background at the start to set the scene. The devil is, of course, in the detail, as a "current position" can be as simple as a list of issues we intend to address, or a complex baseline of our workforce all the way up to individual level.

How to Develop the Plan

People often say to me, "I don't have time to develop a plan". To which I say, "of course you do". Actually, that's not true as you'll generally have to listen to about an hour of talking about how busy they are, and then bring the conversation slowly around to the fact that time is one of three factors: Time, Cost and Quality.

If I asked you to come up with a workforce plan for an Integrated Care System in an hour, you could do it. It would be very low quality, but you could do it. Similarly, you could pay hundreds of thousands of pounds for a beautifully written and developed plan over six months that could be much higher quality.

The trick is to develop something that best balances those three factors. Perhaps something developed over a month, engaging just the right people might produce something that is good enough?

The definition of the quality of the plan is partly set in the previous paragraphs. By engaging the main stakeholders, you can find out how quick it needs to be and what they need. You can also ask them how much cost they are willing to bear in terms of assistance, expenses and disruption to existing teams.

Obviously, there are also different stakeholders with different needs. The Executives of an ICS may want a workforce plan or strategy quickly and with minimal disruption, but you know that service-users and staff will need to be engaged at some point. You can therefore develop an initial plan to secure the investment, and then sort out the detail with much more engagement later on.

The Approach

Building a workforce plan is a project, and as such you can go right back to the approach we set out in the Workforce Redesign part of this book and follow that. Specifically you will:

Mobilise the project: With all of the governance, project charter, stakeholder engagement and planning that entails.

Understand the current state: Everything may need to be on a larger scale and less detailed, but an understanding of the "now" is a part of the plan.

Develop the future state: Using similar engagement techniques, but possibly on a larger scale.

Model the future state: May not be as granular as it would be for a redesign, but modelling is a key part of developing the detail for the document.

Implement the change: Business cases and benefits realisation plans; action plans and communications strategies. You'll need to use all elements of the implementation stage in workforce plan development.

So everything we did in those stages for redesign, we need to do for the project of developing a workforce plan. That includes setting up the governance, project charter, SMART goals, stakeholder engagement and planning in the mobilisation step. It means collecting and presenting data in the current state stage. It means engaging with stakeholders to develop a future state, in a workshop or series of workshops, and it means developing the implementation plan and governance. If you don't know what I'm talking about, then you need to re-read the redesign section.

But I won't leave you there, because this project is different. Yes, we are redesigning the future, but we aren't redesigning individual pathways or teams. By developing a workforce plan or strategy we are saying "we need to redesign these teams, and in this order". It helps place the workforce redesign programmes within a wider narrative and actually make them more likely to succeed. I told you that this was important...

So then, let's consider some specifics for this project.

Engagement

When it comes to developing a high-quality workforce plan quickly, I am a big fan of workshops and other engagement approaches to develop not only the future state, but the current state.

Given that the strategy or plan needs to engage people, one thing that will turn people off is if they see that their particular big issues are not being addressed. Now, I'm not saying that a strategy should just take account of everyone's pet projects, but understanding what everyone thinks are the problems has massive benefits:

First, if they are experts, they are probably right. If someone on the front line tells you that radiology services have a huge backlog and they think the service is going to fall over, then you can be fairly sure that there is an actual issue and 100% sure that there is a perceived issue.

Second, if you talk to lots of people, you develop themes. If one person on the front-line is likely to be right, then getting ten views will help you be much more confident that something is wrong and needs addressing.

Third, even if it turns out that the strategy doesn't address points that people have raised, you can reflect that you heard it, but that it didn't make the cut or was not backed by evidence (and you can go back to people with this feedback before the plan is completed).

Finally, if you've asked people, they can't suddenly say at the end that, "This is rubbish because it doesn't address X". You haven't developed the strategy, WE have. They should have told you when they had the chance.

Taking all of the above, engagement on the current state is, I believe, vital.

The approach that we typically take includes:

Interviewing a lot of people: By sending them a standard agenda of questions, and then having a quick meeting/call to find out what they consider to be the big issues, then you can engage with the individual on a personal basis.

Survey: You can just go with those interviews if you like. If you ask them "What are your top ten issues that need addressing", then you can report on everyone's top issues. But people like to bounce off the views of others, and can't be expected to remember everything. So, I like to send out a summary paper, or even better, a survey (Mentimeter and Survey Monkey both offer free and paid for services). That way, you can get people to vote on the whole, which may prompt people to think wider than their own remit.

Workshops: You can, if you want, skip those steps and just get everyone together in a workshop. You can just ask the question (preferably in groups and with Post-It notes (everyone loves a Post-It note)), "What are the issues". You can then summarise them and get people to vote on them in the session, thus identifying the ones that most people think are an issue. I prefer to do some work up front (for all the reasons I talk about in the redesign section) and to pull together a straw-person view on what the main issues are. I also like to get people to do a PEST or PESTLE analysis.

In the first workshop, all I aim to get to is a prioritised list of issues and solutions, and get groups to have worked up a bit more detail on the issue/solution, where we can get data and who should be involved. Nothing too heavy. Then everyone leaves the first workshop feeling happy. Agreeing who then runs each improvement workstream is then best done outside the workshops. This is difficult, low-energy stuff and isn't really up for group debate, only the sponsors of the project, who are accountable for its delivery, should really be tasked with finding the best people to lead each stream. A second workshop can then engage stakeholders around these leads to get involved in, and inform, more detailed plans.

Quantitative Data

Qualitative data can be enough on its own. In some cases, it's all you can get. We recently did some work in a Cancer Network, and it became clear that the data was so bad that we could not get an accurate picture of the issues with the time and money that we had. We had little choice but to use qualitative data as our only way of identifying issues.

However, quantitative data, even in that example, was still important. We need to look at it for quite a few reasons:

We need to test the hypothesis that comes from the qualitative view: It is possible that, whilst lots of people think radiology is a big problem, it turns out that it isn't that big (spoiler: it is a problem at the moment). It is possible that the workshop was immediately after another one where everyone was discussing radiology. It could be we had a lot of staff from the radiology team in the workshop. Whatever the reason, having a qualitative and quantitative view helps corroborate the findings.

We may find new things: It is possible that we had no cancer team representative, or no-one from care homes or social care in the room (maybe because the team are so stretched they couldn't send anyone to the workshop). You should be able to do a high-level scan of shortages and numbers to identify opportunities or issues that have not been raised. In reality, the qualitative approach should have picked out the main ones, but a quantitative view can and does provide insights.

We need to frame the discussion: We can't run a strategy on hearsay and anecdote. Hang on, what am I saying? Of course we can, we do all the time, but we shouldn't. Once we've established what we are looking at, we need to understand that issue through data. How big is the group? How has demand changed? What are the shortages? Sickness levels? Most of the things we talk about in the baselining section will be relevant here to some extent, so we can collect it and present it to frame the discussion and start to build the case for change. People are more likely to act with some sort of information. The trick here is to create what an old colleague of mine used to call "The Minimum Case for Change", which is just enough to get people to act, not too much that you waste time.

We need to assess the benefits: We need to know that it's all going to add up. If a mental health strategy is being developed against the view that we will need another 10,000 nurses in five years, we'd better make sure that the schemes we are talking about have a fighting chance of getting close. We may deal with issues that are important to other stakeholders that don't help much towards this, but if we don't also make a big dent in that overall number, our internal stakeholders won't fund the work. We also need to create a compelling vision, and benefits data is part of that.

Detail will be needed eventually: Finally, detailed planning will need detailed data so the more we can collect now, the better.

Document and Good Practice Review

Somewhere in the middle is the document review and the good practice from other systems and countries. Again, this is part of the redesign approach and that section is well worth looking at again, because the document review can bring a lot of advantages. Again, HEE STAR is a good place to look, as is the Internet and whatever else people suggest.

A document/good practice review can help by:

Expanding people's thinking: A document review is a great way of identifying models that people might not otherwise consider, which may change where they think we ought to focus. If a new AI algorithm can identify likely issues and thus speed up review of images, that might be a real game-changer, so needs to be in the plan at some point. We've found that presenting these models can change perspectives, but even better, if you can get experts to present and bring the review to life it can yield real benefits:

- When we did this for a mental health study in the North West of England, the local AHSN brought in digital specialists to engage with people in the workshop. This opened the attendees' eyes to what digital solutions were available, and created some digital options that would otherwise not have been considered.
- Similarly, we introduced local people to give presentations on what they had seen and tried.
- Finally, we often introduce a patient view (through a speaker, to augment those working in groups) to provide a viewpoint that the staff don't always see.

Providing indications of issues and solutions from elsewhere: As well as the expansion of views, benchmarking and other documents can highlight where we may also have gaps. As you know, all benchmarking is evil, but it can suggest that there is an opportunity to investigate if our performance is so much worse than others.

Help us understand what will change: The qualitative approach will tell us about the current pressing issues and may give us thoughts of the future if those involved are thinking ahead. But data can really help us quantify what is likely to happen, which may highlight more pressing issues, or suggest that solutions to current issues are just around the corner. Analysis of demand patterns, workforce age (being very careful here around collecting personal characteristics of staff), training numbers, turnover rates, etc. will provide a picture of the future if we don't act, which may be bleaker or rosier than the current one (spoiler: it will probably be bleaker).

Providing potential models for implementation: If one of our ideas is, or involves, the introduction of a new role, a document review can identify if there are already job descriptions, banding, competency frameworks, training guides and anything else you might need. HEE STAR is full of these. Get It Right First Time (GIRFT), NICE and others may have suggested pathways. These will reduce the cost of implementation and provide confidence that these have been tried and/or are working elsewhere.

Future State Planning

You can create a plan in outline that just shows what the problem is, and how we are going to address it, but doesn't get into the detail of the future yet. It says, "this is the problem, and we've kicked off these ten projects that we reckon are going to address it". This could prove a useful document to show that you have a plan, as well as a way of securing the agreement and investment you are going to need, which is vital. You can identify the required benefits for each as part of the project, but not the agreed benefits or the actual changes as these are something that will be determined by the team.

If you are going to take this approach, you could consider doing the following after any workshop:

Making sure there is a named lead for the project.

Assigning (or asking for volunteers for) a team to assist each project.

Developing and supplying a pro-forma for the team to complete (which can then be used in the plan document). You can consider the use of the Project Charter from the redesign section of this book.

Supporting the teams, either in a large-scale workshop, or in individual meetings, to come up with an outline plan for the project. This should include:

- Description.
- Clear scope.
- Links and dependencies to other projects.
- Resources needed.
- Metrics.
- Work already being done.
- Overview plan for the redesign.
- Estimated, targeted benefits and timescales for delivery. This will very much be based on what the project needs to solve, rather than what they agree it will solve, as the redesign hasn't yet been done. However, it sets the expectations on the project, and monitoring and challenge sessions can focus on whether it is on track to address issues.
- Agree the governance as to how progress towards redesign in each of the areas will be monitored and supported.

If you get everyone to do this, it will form your future state, alongside a summary table with associated discussion as to what extent the planned projects are likely to address the issues (and any further work you plan to do to fill any gaps or de-risk the programme).

But you can also create a plan which shows a detailed picture of the future state. Obviously this is the gold standard: A complete record of background, current state, issues, detailed future state (with benefits) and implementation plan.

This will require a redesign project to be undertaken and documented, and for that you have a whole redesign section of the book to help you through...

Summary of Approach

If you put all of this together, the steps included in the WRaPT: Plan approach are typically:

Mobilisation.

Interviews.

Document review.

Initial data analysis.

Develop and send out pre-workshop view on issues and solutions.

Workshop 1:

- Present initial view on issues and solutions.
- Engage patients and local and national experts to present some points of view.
- Get people to do a PEST or PESTLE analysis as a group, using Post-It notes in groups.
- Get people in groups to add their thoughts on what issues and solutions are missing.
- Ask people to prioritise them, either through Mentimeter if online, or through putting stickers on each one.
- Pick out the top solutions and get groups working on developing each:
    - Describe the issue, including estimating its size
    - Identify the data to prove the extent to which this is an issue.
    - Detail how we can solve it.
    - Assess who should be involved in solving it.

Between workshops:

- Present to the steering group/ Executives and check that it is broadly on track to meet requirements.
- Agree main solutions.
- Agree who will lead on planning and implementation of each area.
- Undertake some wider data analysis.

Workshop 2:

- Summarise the main issues and planned solutions.
- Engage patients to present their view again.
- Introduce leads.
- Break into groups with theme leads and discuss:
    - Data sources.
    - Who is going to help.
    - Plan.
    - Project charter.

- Ongoing governance.

After workshops:

- Undertake detailed data analysis around the issues.

- Final planning:

  - Assign a lead and team for each project.

  - Support the teams, either in a large-scale workshop, or in individual meetings, to come up with an outline plan for the project, or to undertake the project and identify a detailed implementation plan.

  - Document the plan (see next section).

If you follow this approach, you should be able to develop a plan of any level of complexity.

Focus: The Politics Problem with the Future

When we talked earlier about why workforce planning was impossible, we mentioned the alignment with finance. Which is a bit unfair on finance, because the issue is a little more complex than that. But finance make such good cartoon baddies... The real trouble is that there is significant pressure for a workforce strategy to (a) actually create a sustainable workforce future, and (b) align with whatever the organisation or system are telling the region or the centre (both from a workforce and a financial viewpoint).

In reality the finance picture isn't going to be real and neither is anything else pulled together to a central timeline. Also, few systems in the current environment are going to produce a workforce plan that immediately (if ever) meets budget and growing demand whilst following safe workforce standards. Massive transformation is needed, which will need all the other stuff we talk about in the, "Why is workforce planning impossible?" section.

As we mentioned there, a possible answer for the future section of a workforce plan is to show all the possible futures, like Greater Manchester did. Show a range of cases: One that matches whatever finance have told regions, others for any other pictures we've provided regionally or nationally, and then a variety of cases to represent what might happen if we implement the plan we've pulled together. Manchester asked a think tank to pull a potential future together, but you could also include best, worse and most likely cases together.

Basically, show all the potential futures on one graph. If you are planning for a single team then it's possible that you can predict an accurate future but once you get to system level, the potential futures are little more than aspirations.

The great thing about including all the futures is that it allows people to have grown up conversations about why they are different, which might mean that people actually work to bring them closer together.

Chapter 3.1

What a Plan Looks Like

So, that last one, "Document the plan". One line, but weeks of effort generally. Remember that a workforce plan is really just:

- *Background and context.*
- *What is currently going on.*
- *What we need to move to.*
- *How we plan to move from where we are to where we are going to.*

So don't let the following list scare you too much, because you don't need to do it all. And of course, you can do as much or as little as your audience needs to make a positive decision on implementing change. A typical strategy or plan that I pull together will include:

Summaries

This document is going to get big, no matter what you do, and people just might not have the time to read. So I always feel that two summaries work:

Executive: One to two pages that pick up a paragraph on background, a summary of issues and the key points for the future with a nod to governance.

Summary: A page for each section, with a bit more information that you can't cram into the executive summary

Then into the main document:

Background

This just needs to include:

- International and national context.
- Local context.
- The reasons for the change.

Current

In this area, any sort of analysis can be included if it is useful, and there were a large range of potential things to include covered in the redesign section. What you include will also depend on the level. You have to go high level if you are looking at a system, whereas you can be very specific for a single team. There are a few key things though that I like to put in a plan:

PEST or PESTLE analysis: We've explained this before, and it is something that you can get a workshop group to complete for you. I like it because it includes strengths you can build on, which can otherwise get missed when you just focus on issues.

Organisation charts: Some sort of view on the organisations that are in the system, or the teams within an organisation. Preferably with a view of how many people are in each one, to give an impression of scale. Showing the fractured nature of some delivery elements (primary care, care homes) and the split between elements like public and private or health and social care. This element can be a powerful driver for change in its own right.

Current staff numbers: A view on the current numbers of people that work in the system or trust, generally broken down by role. Summaries can be numbers by role, with more detailed looks into each role, stats on the number of roles and how many people are in them, the impact of volunteers and carers etc. All of these provide insight into the current team.

Activity: As we've said before, it's all about demand. A view on activity should be a view about the service-user. What is demand (preferably from population health information or similar)? What are activity levels, and what is their trajectory? What is the service-user satisfaction level? What is the difference between commissioned and actual activity?

Staff issue information: This is where we get to highlight the current state of staffing. You have two options here:

- Present a general overview of information that issues can be drawn from, including training rates, sickness levels, bank and agency use, turnover, staff satisfaction, vacancies, full list of issues raised etc. This gives us a picture of the issues that the system faces.

- Pick issues, and dig into them. Alternatively, or in addition, you can highlight some issues and dive deeper into them. Thus as part of the baseline you can say, "The system faces ten key challenges", and then delve into them.

Process/flow: Anything that can show the flow of service-users between organisations or along a process can be useful, although normally more so for individual pathway plans rather than a full system. Understanding how fractured it is, or where the large flows are, can be useful information for stakeholders that should drive organisational change.

Locations and facilities: I don't tend to go overboard on these, but a look at the main locations and how many work in each location can be useful. For a system, this might be a look at the main sites, or for a team it could be locations within a site, but only if it is relevant.

Equipment and IT: To complete the wider view, highlighting the state of equipment and IT that the staff have and associated issues, can be a useful addition to a baseline.

Wider issues: Finally, bring in a list of other issues that the workforce face (generally associated with organisational structures, processes, locations, equipment and IT).

The Future

I like to break this section down into four parts:

One: I start the section with a view on how things will change in the future if we do nothing, this builds on the current state, but shows increases in demand and how staff will change (usually a decrease unfortunately) through the balance of turnover vs recruitment.

At this point in the Hollywood story, we are at rock bottom, having been presented with all the things that need to change and what will happen if we do nothing– but this is as low as we go, as we are now starting to build the glorious future!

Two: And this glorious future starts with the opportunities from good practice, document review and existing models. This is a chance to bring in the opportunities that change could bring.

Three: Then we are in to a picture of

what the future could look like if we implement the changes we want to implement. In reality this is usually a bit of an estimate, and it suffers badly from politics, which we'll talk about in a minute. This is the point at which you can play in any workforce modelling that has already been done (if you have got to that stage).

Four: If I am doing this for a team or pathway, I'll include:

- New process or care model.
- New organisation charts.
- Explanation of new workforce model.
- Workforce model outputs: Future staff and activity numbers.
- New or needed IT and estates changes.

Which is basically the output from the redesign stage (see redesign section). When doing this for a whole organisation or a system then what the future state looks like will probably depend on what level you've taken it to.

It absolutely could be a detailed breakdown of what is changing across the whole system, even down to team level, but that is unlikely. It could be a detailed breakdown of changes across multiple workstreams. Or It could just be a breakdown of potential workstreams.

The Case for Change

Before getting permission to do something about this, we need a compelling case for change. Whilst this is partly in the summary, it is important to end the future section on a high. You are very much at the game show, "This is what you can win" part of the process. We're about to get into the detail of how we are going to make this happen, so we need to be able to make it worthwhile.

The Plan

So, you've got the current state, or "as-is". You've got the future state or "to-be". Now you've got to describe how on this sweet earth you get from one to the other. This section breaks down naturally into:

Description of each of the projects or changes that are going to make this happen:

- Who is involved.
- Description.
- Detailed plan (including Gantt chart or key milestones).
- Expected benefits.
- Assumptions.
- Costs and assistance needed.

Basically, pretty much a project charter (as in the redesign section).

At this point, let's remind ourselves that workforce redesign is about people, so this document needs to be about people: The staff and patients. The current state needs to consider the viewpoints of staff and patients. Descriptions of how we developed the plan need to highlight their pivotal role. And the future state needs to consider how we are engaging those people affected by the change, through consultation.

Implementation approach and governance within organisation: This section of the document should describe how you will ensure that this will be implemented. This should include:

- Details of governance and the steering group (including ToR). This will include how often they will meet, who will meet, who they report to, what their responsibilities are etc. The mobilisation section of the redesign deals with this.
- In many situations, it is unlikely that a plan will completely address the issues. In a health and care system, where organisations are coming together, new digital tools and care models are becoming available and the wonders of population health management are only just starting to be understood, the plan that you pull together will be a step, but not the complete journey. In this case, you will need something more flexible, like a workforce hub or collaborative. We'll cover this in the workforce infrastructure section - a description of this could appear in the plan.
- Details of how the programme will be managed.
- The metrics that will be used (see section on metrics later).

Benefits Plan: Finally, the plan can include the benefits realisation plan which should make a clear link between the overall strategy of the organisation or system, the projects that are being undertaken and the benefits that are expected. Alongside this sits a clear view of those benefits, who owns them, when they expect to be delivered and how they will be delivered.

Appendices

Hey, knock yourself out in this section. I like to add loads, but also like to make it a separate document to avoid too much heft in the main one. I include:

- People that we have engaged.
- Documents/sources reviewed.
- Workshop outputs.
- Data.
- More detail that couldn't be fitted into the main document.

Taken together, this can provide as detailed a plan as should be required. However, there are a couple of things that you might want to consider for large scale changes:

Engagement and consulting documents: Whilst we have mentioned consultation in the plan, for large-scale change, detailed engagement and consultation documents will be needed. Specialist resource is often employed for this.

Business Cases: As covered in the redesign section, business cases can become very complex for large-scale changes, all the way up to large, technical Full Business Cases (FBC). Again, specialist teams are best engaged for this as capacity and skills are both needed.

Bottom-up or detailed workforce model: We discussed workforce modelling in the redesign section. The outcome of modelling could also be included as a separate document as support to the workforce plan.

Developing the Plan

Conclusion

Developing a workforce strategy or plan is just another project, like Workforce Redesign was in the previous chapter. The same requirements, to bring a group of people along with you on a change journey, apply here. The same need to mobilise, understand what is currently going on, agree a future state, model the impact and plan the implementation, apply here.

This section has set out a clear and proven approach to developing a strategy, using the project approach, and including a set of steps that you can follow to develop that plan. This approach works whether you are developing a plan for a single service in one organisation, or are designing a strategy for a ten-locality health & care system. We have used the approach for each of these.

Yet again, the skills of engagement, organisation, programme management, effective document writing, change management, communication and presentation are again going to be important, as they were when undertaking workforce redesign.

So that's a workforce plan or strategy sorted. But that can't be the end of the story as it needs to be implemented and constantly updated. This is where the next section comes in...

SECTION FOUR

WORKFORCE INFRASTRUCTURE AND ENGAGING SUPPORT

So far we have covered the skills needed for redesign, for planning and the documentation of the plan. When we were talking about the plan, we talked about the need for governance of the programme, and for something more flexible than a single programme of change. We can wrap all of this up into a single term:The Workforce Hub. Well, I say single term, but the reality is that there are lots of terms for the same thing. These include:

- Workforce Hub.
- Workforce Collaborative.
- Workforce Development Hub.
- Workforce Planning & Development Hub.
- Centre for Workforce Innovation.

And none of these have the word "people" in the title yet, so I am sure we will be getting some more variations on that theme as these become more popular.

In my experience, workforce hub-type infrastructures are put in place at the same time, or after, the workforce plan. But they could and should be implemented first so as to be the mechanism by which the redesign, and the plan, is prioritised and developed. It should also identify where the resource for its establishment is procured and funded.

This book is about developing skills in workforce planning and providing free tools and techniques that you can use as part of that. This section will set out a model for workforce infrastructure that you can adapt within your organisation or system, and an approach you can take to developing it.

I was lucky enough to be involved in the work with Greater Manchester Devolution during which they built a Workforce Collaborative that is still working well today. Since then NHSI/E have introduced their System Workforce Improvement Model (SWIM). This sets out levels of maturity for workforce improvement across health & care systems, and includes an "operating model for workforce" as one of its elements.

There are many other approaches around, with some focusing more on innovation or education. What we are going to talk about not only exists in real life, but is also being developed at the time of writing to meet a range of issues from many of different viewpoints. As a workforce planner, I approach things from a fairly traditional viewpoint, but I think this creates a solid core around which exciting, patient-focused and innovative workforce conversations can be held, and detail added.

It is important to note that a workforce hub can work at organisational or system level. Its main aim is to consistently generate and deliver against a workforce strategy, and therefore sits as a link between the overall strategy and the front line teams. The examples I will use here are generally for a system (STP, ICS, ICP), as it is more common and complex.

Chapter 4.1

The Workforce Hub Overview

In this section, we will look at the features of a hub in a bit of detail, but before we do, let's summarise what one is and who works in it. First of all, there are a couple of views on this that I have seen already. In some cases the hub is the whole infrastructure, whereas in others, it is the team that helps the Workforce Lead. In reality, it doesn't matter, but I'll describe the whole thing that is needed anyway.

My view of a hub, or collaborative is summed up in the diagram on the following page. It takes many forms, but it is the entity that gets workforce done. It includes the following team:

An Executive Lead or Executive Director. Obviously, this is a critical role as it:

- Sets the ambition for the workforce programme.
- Influences the culture of how the workforce strategy is developed and delivered.
- Is the primary link to ensure that the workforce programme is part of something wider across the system.
- Protects the programme from spurious requests and instead keeps it on track with meeting priorities, in the long term as well as the short term.
- Chairs the People/Workforce Board for the system.
- Seeks to build consensus and engagement across place-based systems, ICPs and key partner organisations.

The Executive Lead for workforce will be part of the overall system board, and will formally update them on the workforce agenda.

A system Workforce Lead: Even a small system will need a Workforce Lead to manage the workforce agenda. Working to the Executive Lead, the Workforce Lead will be responsible for many of the things that the Executive Lead is accountable for. That usually means that they will do most of the work...

A Team: The Workforce Lead may do everything themselves if they are in a small system, but most will have an employed group of people that get things done. They will include:

- ***A Programme Management Office:*** A person, a team or part of a person that does everything to monitor progress.
- ***Administration:*** A function that arranges the complex administrative world of the hub.
- ***Doers:*** There is a problematic term right there, as admin and PMO people do stuff as well. But the doers are those people employed at the core of the collaborative to do stuff. This might be a huge team, or be nobody, depending on the work that needs to be done, and the amount that is done outside of the core team. This is where the rings come in, because in a good hub work will be spread across the various parts of the system.

Place-based, ICP or organisation representatives: The hub needs a mechanism to engage with sub-systems (ICPs) or organisations if it is a small system.

System: The Executive Lead will link into

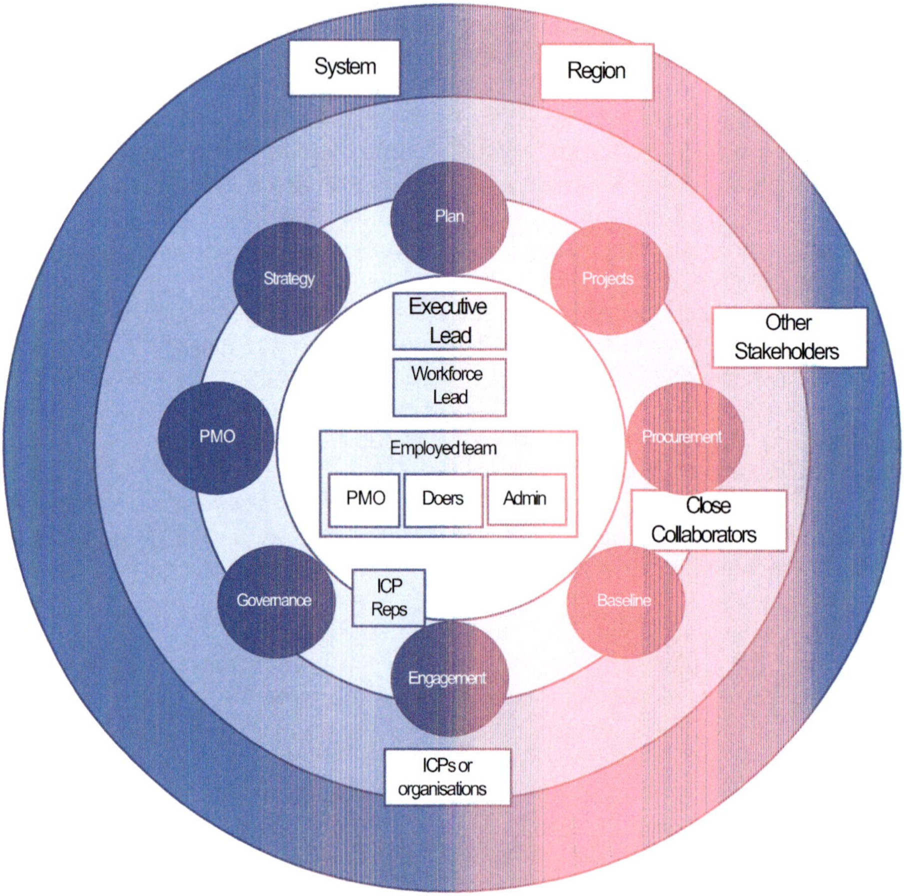

Diagram 2: The Workforce Hub Overview

the overall system governance....

Region: ...and into the regional governance.

ICPs/Organisations: The ICP reps will link with their organisations.

Close collaborators: We'll cover this more under engagement, below, but the collaborative needs collaborators. These can be anyone from workforce or other experts, regulators, staff-side, service-users, volunteers, staff, carers, people in the wider population, private companies, think tanks, basically anyone who is willing to help (or is helping anyway) either unpaid or paid to do so. It is this group that will deliver the workforce programme alongside (or instead of) the core team. It is made up of formal work being commissioned by the programme, work that was going on anyway and a structure for learning from and building on what is happening.

Other stakeholders: And if you aren't directly helping deliver it, you can still be a stakeholder that can inform and engage with the workforce agenda in some way. As we will pick up later, the concentric circles (or rings) show how close these groups are to the core team. The closer you are, the more involvement you have, and the more work you need to do.

Then you come to the dark blue circles, which set out the functions or elements needed in a workforce infrastructure. We'll cover those in the next chapter.

In this model, you can see the hub as the whole people infrastructure (including the People Board and System Workforce Lead) or you can see a hub as an enabling function that supports a wider team.

You can also consider this model at different levels of a system. Regionally, or at STP, ICS and ICP level, you can consider your workforce infrastructure using this model. As you become more regional, you are simply doing more monitoring and assisting than actual doing, but even in the smallest ICP, the job of a workforce hub is to co-ordinate the activity of many people and groups toward meeting the overall goals of the system, not to do everything itself.

But there are absolutely things that it does need to do, as we will see in the next chapter.

Focus: Metrics

One of the roles of the Hub will be to monitor progress against actions. But just because you have completed some actions doesn't necessarily mean that you have done them properly, or that they were the right actions in the first place, or that some other problem hasn't cropped up that has led to the issue getting worse while you were doing the right things. As well as monitoring actions, you need to monitor changes in metrics. But this isn't easy (hey, this is workforce planning, of course it isn't easy). The easy stuff to monitor probably isn't what you want to monitor, so I see lots of pretty graphs being developed that don't help the cause in the slightest.

The list at the end of this section includes some example metrics that you could consider, based around the team itself and the seven R's of workforce planning. Some of these are easy to get from existing sources, whereas others are harder to get and will require new mechanisms for collection. Some are available at summary levels, but might be harder to get for the specific area that you are redesigning.

In order to establish the metrics that you ought to be measuring, you need to consider a logic model that takes you through the thought process from what you are trying to achieve, through to the metrics that you will be monitoring. To do this, the steps and questions could include:

- What is the overall aim of the changes we are making?
- What are the actual individual changes we are making?
- By looking at the changes, what impact do we expect each change to have and what is the overall expected effect?
- What can we measure to show that the change has worked?
- And then:
    - Can we actually use the metrics as part of the redesign, so that it drives ongoing improvement (What gets measured gets managed, as they say. I don't know who they are, but they do apparently say it)?

- What should the reports look like to best show whether this is working?

- How can we accurately and efficiently collect the information?

In this model, the consideration of how easy data is to collect comes last and we don't base our metrics on the available data.

So enough of this process talk, what are the example metrics you might want to collect? Time for two pages of bullet points…

The Team: This is the only set not related to the seven R's as it relates to the team as it is at the moment, not how we fill gaps between demand and capacity. Example metrics include:

- Vacancies.
- Gap between demand and capacity.
- Bank and agency.
- Staff satisfaction.
- Diversity of the team.
- Activity per person.

Recruit: Hiring people into the team:

- Recruitment versus plan.
- Candidate conversation (to measure the effectiveness of initial screening, or to measure how engaging the process is.
- Hire to reach productivity time (as in, how long does it take to get the recruit up to full speed).
- Diversity of recruit pool (and potentially comparison with how many make it to offer).
- Cost per hire.
- Candidate satisfaction (both those that succeed and those that do not get the post).

Retain: Keeping staff from leaving:

- Turnover/Retention rates.
- Employees recommend as great place to work.
- Ease of access to employee benefits (or rate of take-up of benefits).
- Last time employee was recognised.
- Internal hiring mechanism effectiveness.
- High potential people (HiPo) in voluntary turnover.
- Diversity of turnover.

Retrain: Developing skills to fill scarce roles:

- Impact of training after 30 days.
- Learning & Development (L&D) Participation.
- L&D Return on investment (RoI).
- Skills matrix improvement.
- Training backlog.

Return: Getting people to return to work after retirement or leaving:

- Number of returners.
- % Of retirees who undertook return planning.
- Reason for return.

Redesign: Transforming roles:

- Action Progress versus plan (making sure that the steps have been taken).
- Productivity after change (checking that the benefits have been received).

- Change progress/completed (identifying how many changes have actually been implemented).

- New role staff feedback.

Re-energise: Getting more work done with the current team:

- Job planning inaccuracies (very specifically measuring things like consultant job-plan variance, rostering lost time due to failing to fill contracts or time when staff were not productive due to having no work to do, such as clinics cancelled, demand below expectations, lists finished early due to not enough cased being listed, etc).

- Non-productive effort.

- Absence.

- Long term absence.

- Wellness (I'm not sure quite how you measure this, but it is important. It will probably be through surveys…).

Replace: Reducing the need for staff through changes (e.g. digital):

- Impact of change (checking that the technology actually does reduce the amount of time expected).

- % of staff redeployed to other useful roles.

- Employability of exiting workers (measuring how flexible staff can be to move to other roles, should automation replace their current roles).

That is quite a list, but it can be made longer, as many of these metrics can be considered through a range of different lenses:

- Versus plan.

- Overall numbers.

- By type of staff.

- By grade.

- By organisation.

- With a focus on specific ones.

Have fun coming up with metrics for your programme. I am sure that there are many more that you can add to this.

Chapter 4.2

Workforce Hub Roles

The dark blue circles on the earlier diagram set out the main roles or task groups for the hub. The document seems to have lot of blue circles on it, so you are looking for the smaller, dark blue ones). You'd think I could have used different colours…?

Let's consider each of these in turn:

Strategy

It needs to set the workforce strategy. This is done using the approach we have set out in section three and provides a clear vision that everything else can work towards. Of course, if the strategy exists, the hub can merely take this and implement it, or can work to enhance it if needed.

The hub is, as we have discussed, mainly a co-ordinator of activity – it can't do everything…

Plan

It does though need to write and hold the workforce plan, including a detailed set of actions that will deliver the strategy. As we discussed in section three, it is probable that you won't have a complete workforce plan as you will really only have identified a set of redesign and other projects that will move us from the current to the future state. As these projects get into their implementation stages (as set out in section two, their plans will update the workforce plan. But you might have completed your redesigns and have a set of implementations to deliver.

Projects or Themes

The redesign, implementation or other projects all need to be delivered. Each should have a plan, owner, team, budget and expectation of benefits (amongst other things as we discussed in section three earlier). If we don't have a plan, or an owner or anything substantial, then this is something that we will need to procure. We'll talk about that later.

Now, this is where it gets complicated, because there are quite a few areas:

Redesign projects: For a health and care system there are a range of current problems that we know need workforce redesign: Elderly Care, Cancer, Mental Health, Radiology, Primary Care etc.

Themes: There are a range of themes which the national People Plan has identified as areas that need focus: Diversity, making the NHS a great place to work, redesign etc. These themes need to be addressed, and may form part of the strategy, but may not yet have a full range of projects developed. Many hubs have a lead for various themes.

Theme projects: Individual projects may be developed and initiated by theme leads.

Other central projects and work: Specific work will be ongoing to increase (normally) the number of staff in needed roles. This will include recruitment actions, retention actions and actions around many of the other R's.

Other local projects and work: In a system, there are multiple organisations that will be undertaking a range of projects and work that may help towards the delivery of the strategy. The hub will need to be able to work to help identify what is helping and what can be shared across the whole system. As a collaborative organisation, a hub is rarely in a position to stop extraneous activity, but it can perhaps highlight this.

Procurement

Not all projects that are needed will be delivered immediately. The strategy will have prioritised areas that require adjusting, and national or regional pressures may introduce additional activity that is needed. The hub should aim to procure projects that need to be delivered quickly, either from organisations within the system, or from contractors of some sort, generally within the scope of those we are engaging with as a collaborative.

If we have a whole lot of stuff to do, and we can't do it ourselves, we have a choice: We can seek funding for it elsewhere (which we can then use to pay others to do the work, or to build our own capability); we can find the money ourselves; or we can do it with the scarce resources we do have, possibly by getting one part of the system to deliver it, and then sharing the learning.

Whatever way we choose, we need a system to identify priorities, identify options for getting those priorities delivered, and a mechanism for procuring the resources to deliver it. A good function will be watching for funding or free assistance opportunities that national bodies offer. For example, if HEE are offering free Star training, can we use that to help us with our capability issue?

The hub function will need a clear process for highlighting where work needs to be done and finding the right people to deliver it. They will also need a function for hearing "pitches" from people asking for funding to deliver something that will be useful. A good process will include:

Development of the market: So that the team are aware of potential suppliers and that those suppliers are aware of the needs of the system (see engagement, later), we need to engage with potential suppliers, and help them understand the capacity we need.

Recording and reporting on gaps that may require assistance.

Advertising gaps and requesting offers of help.

Recording of responses.

Development of a set of options for consideration.

Process of engagement with the People Board to agree best options: This can be quite complicated, because lots of people want to have a view on how money is spent, but you don't want to spend the whole time talking about this at People Board. I'd suggest a sub-committee to meet regularly to undertake this work and then report to the People Board.

A process for handling offers of help not associated with issues will be needed, which will generally consist of meeting the people, understanding the offer, shortlisting a few for discussion and then getting them to pitch at the sub-committee.

Finally, delivery needs to be managed: But that is elsewhere in the responsibilities.

Baseline

The strategy and plan will include some sort of baseline information as part of the case, and every redesign project will need information on the current state. It is therefore worthwhile for a hub to maintain a single baseline view for use in these projects.

There is also a reality that regional and national bodies have a voracious appetite for information of various sorts, and the hub can take on the role of handling and fulfilling those requests, for a view on the current and future predictions for staffing levels of various groups. In order to do this, it needs to make a decision as to whether:

- It seeks to hold a complete view of each organisation's current and planned future workforce, constantly keeping this up to date in some sort of data warehouse or similar.

Or...

- It builds a system for quickly getting the information from organisations when required.

As we have mentioned, SWIM sets out a maturity model, and this is an area where maturity is going to take time for any region. When we are working in a hub, maturity looks like evolving along the following lines:

Pull together what you can find: This is where we start, pulling together a view on the current staff situation, issues and any information on planned changes. This is a great job to get the collaborative involved in, because there is a huge amount of information out there, it's just not well curated in most cases.

Start to develop relevant sources: Once you've done the trawling for what is out there, and then curated it so that the next time you, or anyone else, looks to do it they have a trail of breadcrumbs to follow, you need to develop new sources.

This is where it gets unpopular with the front-line teams, because you need to start requesting information from people. Of course for that reason it is highly popular with people in the centre because they can just send off spreadsheets and get someone else to do all the work (see section on data requests earlier for hints and tips on how to annoy people). Until they find that nobody is replying...

The trouble is that we need this data to answer questions we and others have, so these sources need to be developed, and then maintained so that we can actually answer them.

Consider a system: The above approach is painful, because there is no standard mechanism for people to record all the information we need. The Electronic Staff Record (ESR) in Trusts often holds most of the current numbers etc, but doesn't have every piece of information we have asked for about the current state, let alone people's workforce plans.

It was partly for this reason that WRaPT was developed in the first place, although it quickly became clear that not many people actually cared that they weren't actually workforce planning. The WRaPT team talk quite a lot now to systems that are looking to find ways of holding information on baselines and plans at team and organisation level, and whilst WRaPT may not have all the answers, it can be part of an overall solution. As can other, more manual, approaches.

Build a single information repository: Finally, we know of at least one system that is actively developing a single system for the holding of baseline staffing information and planned new staffing models, but this is likely to be outside the ambitions of all but the largest systems.

I have deliberately not mentioned the "just make it up to match the finance information", which we don't recommend, but is quite possibly the most popular...

Capacity

The whole point of this book is that there aren't enough people with enough skills and experience in workforce planning and redesign across the health & social care system. It therefore makes sense for the hub to focus on building the skills, experience, tools and techniques in the right people so that workforce planning becomes a much more common occurrence. With the sheer amount of work that needs doing, building the capacity will ensure that more can get done better and faster, and without having to bring in too much outside assistance.

Within this element, there are a few areas to consider:

Identifying a set of tools and techniques that will form the basic approach for the system: We can identify a set of workforce planning techniques, redesign techniques, modelling tools etc. that we will invest in. That doesn't mean that people can't use other tools as the job is so large it seems churlish to restrict them if they have a favourite approach or already have skills. But building a standard vocabulary for the system or organisation allows everyone to start building a language for workforce planning. These might be the approaches we invest in, but central entities often provide funding for new and innovative approaches, and it is always worth taking this help when it is offered.

Training people in these approaches: Which you can do through e-learning, but there is a lot more to be said for training groups of people and using action learning while they are undertaking practice projects. As we have discussed before, this makes the training relevant to the large challenge, provides experience and successes. Building a development programme could be a core part of the hub, pulling on the skills and experience of other collaborators. Other areas are going further and developing learning academies and formal university courses.

This function can also consider the use of the approaches in this book for large-scale engagement of people in the system from the front line managers to the system workforce leads.

Engagement

We can talk about engagement from a lot of different viewpoints, making this one of the focus areas of an excellent hub. I split the engagement up into four groups:

Staff, service-users, volunteers, carers, unions etc: These are the people that are involved in the workforce, on the demand and the supply side. They are the people who will be most affected by change, and are the ones most feeling the impact of the current issues. We have talked before about the engagement of service-users, and the need to ensure that engagement is meaningful and broad enough, avoiding the issues that come with token involvement of patients with one issue. The same is true of staff and union engagement: You need to engage a representative group with a broad viewpoint. Engaging service-users, volunteers and carers is an area where getting experts to help can really play dividends. I was lucky enough to work with a great team at HealthWatch Sheffield for many years. They would be in the engagement group from day one if I was setting up a hub over there.

Similarly, engaging staff-side representatives or the Local Medical Council (LMC) can not only help the engagement and improve the chance of delivery, but improve the quality of plans. There can be politics involved with many of these groups (like any organisation), so the engagement should be done mindfully and in discussion with local leaders to select the right teams.

Population: The population is made up of potential service-users and staff, and is therefore a powerful set of stakeholders. Engaging them in workforce redesign from the start can be very valuable and insightful, and major changes are going to need their consultation. And their Consultation (note the capital "C" there) as part of the business case and implementation process. Engaging the population helps us focus on providing what the population needs and wants and what it is going to get, not on what we often focus on, which is what it is going to lose. Removing an A&E Department is never going to be popular. Moving vascular services thirty miles away from the city is never going to be popular. A new integrated service, championed by local leaders and staff which will lead to better outcomes, well it still might not be popular, let's face it, but it might be less unpopular....

Engaging local leaders as well as the overall population can be a part of the hub duties, as can undertaking large scale pieces of engagement work through focus groups, surveys, even buses that travel round engaging the population. This is another area where engaging experts with a track record in delivering this stuff can be beneficial, either to deliver or advise the hub.

Arms Length Bodies (ALB), experts: There are a lot of people out there who want to help, and have something to contribute. Some of these are public bodies with free expertise, and sometimes even have funding that can add to the pot. Some of these can be the regulators, as well as helpers and sourcing of funding. Others are private or public/private entities that can provide training, advice or capacity to deliver the work needed. Organisations that you may seek to include in this are HEE, NHSI/E, Skills for Care, Skills for Health, Leadership Academy, the local AHSN, a local think tank, the WRaPT or local workforce skills development team, some regional representatives, and a chosen support provider.

ICPs/Organisations: The system may be a single system, or include sub-systems, like ICPs. It will certainly include a range of organisations that deliver care (care homes, primary care providers, secondary care providers, tertiary care providers, ambulance trusts, community care providers, mental health trusts, councils, local authorities, and private providers). Many of these will be represented in the governance structure, but they do also need to be engaged.

One of the key reasons for engagement here, especially as systems are forming, is that a lot of the responsibility for action falls on these entities. There is an ongoing need to engage with each organisation, through the various sub systems (like ICPs) to understand their workforce (for baselines and reporting), their issues (for priorities and plans), their actions (as they may be addressing overall system priorities) and their resources (as they may be able to help).

And, please ensure equality, diversity and inclusion in all parts of engagement. I tend to engage expert help here as well.

But, what does this engagement look like I hear you ask. Well, luckily I thought you'd say that. The hub should consider engagement on three levels:

Specific purposes: There will be specific reasons to engage each of these entities. They could be part of the governance structure (see next bit) or they may require engagement as part of redesign programmes or development of the plan or strategy.

The "rings": The above is all a bit ad-hoc and is very driven by individual circumstances. The hub, or in this case should I say collaborative, has the chance to engage people in a much more groovy way, by bringing them into a community of information exchange and discussion. I call this the rings, because of the approach that Manchester developed, that I very much liked. You can ask people where they would like to sit on a series of concentric rings, and set out the offer and the ask. People that are in the inner circle will need to dedicate more time to the enterprise, but by doing so they will be involved more regularly and for longer than those that don't dedicate much time. You can have as many rings as you want, but let's consider the following three ring model:

Inner circle: This group may meet monthly, and be engaged in procurement, prioritisation, problem solving of new issues etc. Their expertise will be used to help manage the agenda, and they may be asked to help out to undertake tasks between meetings. With great power comes great responsibility…

Middle circle: This group may meet quarterly as part of a formal engagement and discussion group.

Outer circle: This group may be engaged annually as part of a large-scale workshop where progress is highlighted, and groups are engaged in discussing various topics, and in future scanning activities.

One thing you need to consider in the largest systems is where this operates. In a large ICS, for example, you may have five ICPs. Do you want this to happen at ICP or ICS level? The answer is, almost certainly, it depends. And, both, as some organisations will not want to engage across five areas, whereas others might.

The plan: Finally, engagement needs to be turned into a deliverable process. We need to know who the groups are, when we are going to communicate with them and what the purpose of the communication is. We need to plan and deliver monthly, quarterly and annual engagement events with the right stakeholders. All of this is a part of the hub's responsibilities or focus. See the earlier section on redesign for discussion about communication plans. This book is big enough as it is without repeating all that again…

Governance

The governance of the workforce programme is critical (isn't everything?). It connects the work being done to the leadership of the system, and if done well it is the route for the system to have confidence in the workforce programme, for the showering of extensive budget on workforce projects and for the integration of workforce redesign with a clear system wide programme of transformation. In reality it will probably at least start with a mind numbing set of confusing meetings with a revolving set of participants who'll spend half the time disagreeing about whether we call people patients, citizens or service-users.

But let's assume we are heading for the sunlit uplands of the first of those scenarios. What do we need for governance?

There are few elements you need:

An Executive Lead for workforce: This person will be accountable for the development and delivery of the workforce agenda and should have been appointed as part of the overall system governance. If you don't have one of these in place then you really are starting from square one.

The Executive Lead should report into and be part of this wider system governance: This would probably involve some of overall system board. In addition, they should report into wider groups, such as a Regional People Board. Their role should be documented in the Terms of Reference of these groups. They will bring strategic challenges to the People Board from these groups, and will expect help in addressing workforce challenges in return.

A mechanism to develop and deliver the workforce agenda: This is typically done through some sort of board such as a Workforce or People Board. This Board will typically include:

- A Workforce Lead, who manages a lot of the day to day work for the Exec Lead and who can link to the workforce hub or collaborative team to undertake required actions.
- The PMO lead, for reporting.
- An administrator, for the agenda and minutes.
- Leads from each of either the sub-systems (ICPs) or organisations in the system (if it is a small one).
- Leads from various specialist groups that support the delivery of the programme.
- Leads from sub-committees to the programme.
- Other stakeholders, including:
    - Staff side or union representatives.
    - Patient, volunteer and carer representatives.
    - NHSI/E.
    - HEE.
    - Others as appropriate.

The People Board will need appropriate Terms of Reference, and a membership that does not rotate: It should include named leads and deputies from each of the groups, and this roster should remain in place as much as possible. Its timing will need to fit with the reporting needs into the System and Regional Boards.

There will need to be links into the ICP

Workforce Groups: A lead for each of these will be on the People Board. Should this be a small system, it will require a lead from each of the organisations, or groups of organisations that make up the system. The ICP workforce groups represent a chance for there to be many and varied flavours of system operation as we have already discussed. Some systems may be ICS focused, whereas others may mainly be led by their ICPs, but the reality is that some work will be done at ICP and some at ICS level no matter what sort of model you follow.

ICP workforce groups should include:

- ICP Workforce Lead and Deputy.
- Administration support, which may also include an element of PMO support.
- Hospital Trust Leads.
- Primary Care Leads (or representative).
- Council/Local Authority Leads.
- Private Care Leads (or representative).
- Mental Health Provider Leads.
- Other key provider leads.
- Primary Care Training Hub Leads.
- Specialists as required.
- Regulators or collaborators as required (HEE, NHSI/E, others).
- Volunteer, carer, patient reps.
- Staff-side or trade union reps.

Although, again, this may not all be in one Board, but may be in a set of sub-groups and supporting collaboratives depending on size. All these groups will need their Terms of Reference, and will need to link with their ICP (or organisation) system boards. This all sounds a bit bureaucratic, but organisations, ICPs and the ICS all have their own accountability for workforce which needs to sit within their overall accountabilities.

Matching all the meeting dates and times to feed into and out of these various committees can be a really fun job. I remember when I was asked to help develop a workforce strategy in two months for one system, I had to point out that we'd already missed the time for papers to go to a subcommittee that needed to review parts of it. Who reads papers anyway....?

There will need to be links with specialist groups that support the People Board: There could be all sorts of these, depending on what you already have set up.

Finally, there will need to be links with the sub-committees: These can be permanent or ad-hoc depending on what needs to happen. Procurement sub-committees may be one, but you may also have ones to deal with developing the strategy, developing workforce capacity or dealing with big workforce challenges.

Keeping the governance working is complex, and isn't easy. I may have made this point before, but nothing with workforce planning ever is...

Programme Management (PMO)

Finally, we are on to the excitement of the PMO or Programme Management Office. A PMO is essentially a mechanism for monitoring and reporting on progress, and driving the actions that should unblock issues and ensure that projects are delivered. You could write a book on developing a PMO, the roles that are needed and the various tools and approaches that you can use, but at its heart it is very simple. The PMO:

Understands the job that needs to be done and when it needs to be done by.

Documents all the things that are being done to address the need, when they are being done and who is doing it.

Highlights variances between the vision, and the actions that are being taken.

Identifies the metrics that need to be monitored to evidence that actions are having the impact.

Measures progress against actions, and improvement against metrics (see the note on metrics below).

Provides reports to the People Board, requests actions and updates them on progress.

The PMO does all of this largely by maintaining control over the whole process, and getting this right requires a strong PMO Manager or Lead, appropriate resourcing and status for the team, strong leadership from the senior People Lead for the system and that the information produced actually be used as part of the governance process. The PMO is a sort of Police Officer, in that it is there to help, and there to flag up where things aren't going right. And could benefit from being equipped with a taser.

A good PMO can also provide the full support to the governance process, making sure that everything gets done, so it can also:

Ensure that the governance meetings happen, are minuted and that actions are chased before the next meeting and reported on (enforcing effective use of meetings).

Manages the procurement and pitching process to ensure that the procurement sub-committee sees the right information, and follows up on its actions. Part of this includes maintaining an effective picture of available budgets.

Organises the various engagement events and report against progress on the communication plan.

Is part of the central operational team.

Manages development of the plan and strategy, as well as the definition of projects.

And if you think that is a stretch, well my benchmark for excellent PMO performance was in Manchester, and the PMO lead there did all of this if my memory serves, and they did it well.

Focus: Baselines and Future State Repositories

CURRENT STATE BASELINES

Earlier in this book, in the redesign section we looked at data and at developing a Current State. Any elements from the data list can be used as part of a baseline.

Baselines are valuable things in their own right, because there are lots of reasons when they might come in handy, even if you are confident that your current situation is perfect.

Reasons include:

To respond quickly and efficiently to data requests: You get these regularly from all sorts of places - regional and national bodies, from the STP/ICS/ICP, regulators or from somewhere in your organisation. In these cases, you are often expected to be able to quickly respond with a current picture: How many people, how many vacancies, how many in specific roles etc. It saves time and effort if you maintain that picture.

For a strategy or plan: The baseline or current state is often one of the early chapters of a plan, as well as providing narrative and scale. Building a baseline provides you with the background on your workforce (size, issues etc) as well as helping to provide the case for change.

You can use it to evidence why things are as they are, or why they need to change: There is often conflict between stakeholders who want things cheaper (let's go with the stereotype and call this "finance"), and those who want more resources to deliver high quality services or make life better for the team ("operations"). A clear baseline that shows how things currently work, can be used to either evidence that the situation is perfect, or point out where it needs to change, so you can get some investment in making the change happen. This is rarely done but is incredibly powerful.

To use as information in undertaking a redesign: Getting stakeholders on board with what is good, and what needs to change, so you can drive discussions about how to change and what to change to.

The reason why you are creating a baseline will drive what sort of product you create:

Regular requests: If you are getting constant requests from the centre, then you need some sort of data repository that you can regularly draw on. This can either be held centrally somewhere or can be a virtual one. A virtual version could be a clear mechanism to get the information quickly from source systems or organisations. Thus, if you are in an organisation that regularly needs to respond, you can either build and maintain a picture for the organisation or have a clear process to ask for and receive this data from the divisions, directorates or teams.

Communication: You may need a more explanatory document, either one that can be used to engage people in the strategy or insightful analysis that points the way towards the areas that need redesigning/or provides the case for change. A baseline like this fits well within a strategy document or plan, explaining the current situation in terms of what you have, as well as where things might need to change.

Analysis model: Finally, you may need a detailed model of workforce and activity that can be used for analysis. For this, we tend to use the WRaPT tool. Whilst WRaPT can be used as a data repository, its real strength comes from being used as a powerful model for analysis. A WRaPT baseline shows the link between workforce, activity and drivers. This can be combined with other baselines, like vacancies, processes etc. Excel, Apex Insight and other tools can also be used for this purpose.

FUTURE STATE

As with the current state baseline, there are three main uses for a future state output:

Data requests: People at the centre and in the regions want to know what your plans are. They will want to get detailed information on how many people you plan to have in the future, and in reality they will want confidence that you have a plan and how you will achieve it. They will combine this with other systems' view, so they will likely be in a standard format, which can be quantitative and qualitative.

A strategy or STP level plan: Those at STP, ICS, ICP level will need something that describes the future for them. They already have a picture of the current state, they now need to understand the future.

Redesign: Finally, and more of a meso- or micro-level view, you may need a future state for a redesign. If you are planning to change stroke services for example, again alongside the baseline data you will need that future state for the model: How the process, structure, locations and digital ways of working have changed. And then how the workforce will change, including how will numbers change, are there new roles etc?

The outputs can be:

Data repository: Like with the current state, a clear picture on the future state will either need to be held centrally or collected from individual organisations via a clear and documented process. Just imagine what it is like sitting at ICS level and getting constant different data requests. You either need that at your fingertips, or you need to have an engaged set of people ready to help you by providing data quickly.

Explanatory document: Again, there are two types here: A quick and engaging view on what the future workforce looks like; or the detail of the future picture for the plan. This will be in two parts:

- ***Model:*** Modelled staff picture of the future, taking into account a transformed process and workforce potentially.

- ***Responses:*** The future for the rest of it: How is this STP or team going to be a great place to work, what are we doing about wellness, talent management, leadership development etc?

Detailed model for analysis: Finally, you need a detailed workforce model, in a tool like WRaPT or Excel. This will drive the benefits model, evidence your future state and provide a model for further amendment should it be required.

Workforce Infrastructure Conclusion

Hopefully, that section gave you an overview of what a Workforce Hub or Collaborative can include, and what it needs to do. This is an area that is obviously important for systems and, as these develop there will be a lot of consideration given to the balance between place, system and regional structures. Each level needs some sort of infrastructure. The rule of thumb should be to do only what makes sense at that level. This would generally include the things that are most important to it, and are worth doing once across a whole region, system or place.

I talk a lot about system, but this is also useful when talking about individual teams, practices, directorates, divisions, departments or organisations. In order to maintain workforce planning (which, as we said right at the start is never complete, it is always needed), a form of hub, even if it is just a quarterly meeting, allows you to do all sorts of useful things: Find funding, prioritise actions, monitor metrics, initiate redesign programmes, monitor implementations etc.

Anyway, that's your lot on the system-level stuff. Now onto the other end of the spectrum, the operational workforce planning skills needed for front-line staff…

SECTION FIVE

OPERATIONAL WORKFORCE PLANNING

Operational Workforce Management is all the things you do with teams and people right up to doing your regular annual planning, or ad-hoc workforce redesign programmes. It's the short-term stuff: The daily, weekly and monthly actions. Lots of skills are useful, but the ones we will cover here are ones that will specifically be needed by the front-line team manager to optimise the use of their team when aiming to meet the demand from service-users. That all sounds a bit cold, but is essentially what workforce planning is. That doesn't mean that you can't make sure that everyone has fun doing it, especially as people that are having fun will work harder and perform better for your service-users….

The reality is that you can do all the things we have already talked about in this book: You've redesigned roles, optimised processes and brought in some new digital solutions to create an efficient and user-focused team. But the job of workforce planning is never-ending. You can't just do it once and forget about it for a year until the next planning cycle. You need to do it all the time.

To do that you need the skills that allow you to operate as an effective leader and manager of people on a week-by-week, day-by-day and even hour-by-hour timeline. The sorts of skills you will need for this include:

Leadership: Being a great leader will help you recruit people, retain people, develop people and get the most out of people. There is a good meme in which a manager is saying "we're focusing on wellbeing", and when the staff reply, "ah great, so you're going to improve working conditions and pay fairly" the response is "we were thinking more of yoga classes". Wellbeing requirements for your team change with the person and with time, so knowing what is important to your team and meeting their needs, is important. Regular, good feedback is more important to some than money at certain points in their career.

Coaching/mentoring: Having the skills to help people develop themselves, as well as using your experience to help them develop, will help ensure that you have a dynamic group, growing into new roles.

Scheduling: Your staff numbers will be based on matching people to the demand coming through the door. If you can do this well, then you will avoid too many situations where demand outstrips supply, which tires staff, reduces outcomes and/or results in overspends.

Managing time and attendance: Your staff actually need to be in work for the new model to work. Being able to manage time and attendance, including maintaining flexibility in your team to cover short term demand, helps you match people to ***demand.***

Managing sickness: Your models will be based on assumptions for absence, so you need to be able to at least meet that. Handling short-term and long-term absence through process and leadership is a required skillset.

HR Process and policy: Knowing the requirements of the law, and the organisation, is important.

Managing activity and team to budget: I've left this one until nearly last, but it is absolutely vital for a manager. Being able to manage a budget in the face of fluctuating (largely growing) demand is important. I see too many managers that don't understand a budget. I see more that do and just let budgets whizz by as demand increases, without understanding the impact that demand has had on their costs. The best manager I ever worked for clearly understood and modelled the impact of demand, and was able to protect the team from cuts, from criticism and from outside interference, as a result.

A whole lot of other skills: These can fit into the leadership bucket but are worth being explicit about. Managing people means managing conflict, showing empathy, applying common sense and judgement and bringing the best out of people. Building your "softer" skills to be a better manager is a process worth undertaking.

Now, we can look at each of these skills individually, and improve our understanding of each. And we will do that. But before we do, let's remind ourselves about the approach to development.

Yes, we need training in this, we need tools and approaches that we can follow. But we also need to engage the organisation in this, and we need practice, and there is no better way than through running a divisional or organisation wide project on this. So, the next chapter will take you through the sort of project that I often get involved in: An organisation-wide approach to developing skills in workforce planning, to meet an Executive-level challenge. It might feel a bit strange to talk about this, when we are discussing short-term skills, but if you want investment (time and money) in developing workforce planning skills, it really only works if you can get permission from your organisation to do it.

Even if you aren't planning an organisation-wide approach, and just want to learn some skills, it's worth a read of the next chapter, to pick up relevant elements of making this fit your organisation's strategy.

Chapter 5.1

Operational Workforce Planning Project

An operational workforce project should really focus on a problem, and preferably one that is a problem for the Executive Team, which means you will get their buy-in to solve it, and it should also link nicely to the strategy. This could include:

Reducing, or controlling cost: For years, before workforce became so scarce as set against demand that suddenly the health of the magic money tree didn't matter, cost was king. Everyone was developing Cost Improvement Plans (CIPs) or similar. With staff at circa 70% of budget, workforce planning can be used as a mechanism to manage cost.

Workforce planning. I have been asked to assist Trusts specifically with workforce planning, where the executive team have been worried about staff numbers and high levels of dependence on dwindling nursing and medical roles. Just having an overall workforce plan is a valuable outcome in its own right (and finance will also want to link it to cost...).

Building operational controls: When people come into the NHS from the private sector, they are often somewhere between worried and horrified with the lack of perceived operational control, as it can be very different from what they are used to. In addition, central drives for Foundation Trust status or similar can also require organisations to have certain approaches embedded (e.g. Service Line Management).

Customer service and quality: Lower staff numbers than demand levels often lead to a lack of access, poorer outcomes and reduced patient or service-user satisfaction. As a result, an organisation-wide programme of workforce planning can be instituted that relies on improving operational workforce control.

Most of these projects include some workforce redesign alongside the improvement in operational people management, because there tends to be opportunity to redesign at the same time, and that all fits neatly into a programme. Workforce redesign skills should be in the toolkit of frontline managers anyway.

So this section will focus on a project that develops the skills of managers, whilst solving a real problem. Going back to that pyramid or tetrahedron that we discussed way back at the start of this unnecessarily long book, we learned that we need to make this important to the organisation if we are going to make workforce planning sustainable.

All of us I am sure have worked on training programmes that have been going swimmingly, until some major programme has swept away any chance of completing it, before we managed to get the development firmly implanted within the organisation or system. I've also worked on programmes where the development has still been going on after eight years, with an engaged executive that understands that the work is continuing to help them meet their objectives. It comes down to it being important to the organisation so that development will be massively benefited by a project, such as I'll set out here.

The project will go something like this:

- Scope & Mobilise.
- Understand current state.
- Design the future state.
- Model the future state.
- Plan and implement.

Well, that seems familiar as it's the standard generic approach again, and that's because it is a project and it should be handled as such. Of course, the detail is a little different, but the steps remain the same.

Scope & Mobilise

So, I've told you that the project needs to be embedded within the organisation. This needs to be important to the top levels of the organisation if it is going to be sustained. The project is going to take somewhere between six months and two years, and in that time lots of other important things are going to pop up that need sorting, so this project needs to be important enough to be sustained. That means it must initially look like it can solve a real problem, and then quickly start proving that it is solving it.

Everything we do surrounding this problem needs to be big, relevant, strategic and important.

You'll remember from the redesign section that there are four steps to mobilising a project:

- Develop the challenge.
- Engage stakeholders.
- Agree project charter.
- Ensure appropriate information governance.

This is all relevant here, but there are some specific things to consider for this type of project in a couple of the areas:

Develop the challenge: When developing the challenge, you need to consider the Board level challenge, as we have just set out. Is this for workforce planning, cost reduction, customer service or for operational control? What benefits are needed? When are they needed by? The challenge is always important, especially so in this case as it will need to be impactful enough to drive and sustain organisational change.

Engage stakeholders: If I was to be honest here, I've messed this sort of programme up quite a few times. In one case it was quite catastrophic for the programme. I was looking to get organisational workforce planning in place and worked with the Executive Lead and his team to develop the approach. What I didn't do was engage the Divisional Teams in what we were doing, and the result was a wall of resistance to the programme that stifled it from the start. That wasn't their fault , it was mine, and it was all due to not engaging the right people.

It was a basic error, but always reminds me that in this sort of programme, you need to include representation from everyone from the front-line all the way down to the Executive.

Another learning point is that you don't always need patient engagement here (although it helps), but you absolutely need staff-side engagement.

Agree project charter: Part of this is developing a plan, so we need to know what this sort of project looks like.

As we have said, this starts with a challenge. Let's take an example from my past, and say that this is about achieving financial balance in a trust's directorates and divisions by making sure that they are all planning their workforce effectively. This will involve developing skills in operational workforce planning, redesign and probably a bit of financial management as well.

This sort of project will include the following elements:

- Data analysis to work out where the biggest problems are.
- Skills analysis to work out who needs training in what.
- Designing an impactful training programme.
- Monitoring success.
- Developing the monitoring and reporting into the Executive.
- Implementation.
- Supporting change.
- Building links into central functions.

The group: The group we are looking at here can be complex. In theory, most health organisations should have a triumvirate approach with a medic, a nurse (or AHP or other non-medical clinician) and a manager. These three should work together to make sure that the team is well run. In theory. And it is a good theory, because if you can get all that lot working together then that would be wonderful. In real life, often one person or role takes control through situational or personal power, and that can be okay too if everyone gets their say and the leader doesn't push forward their own agenda to the detriment of others. So when we are looking at the group whose skills we will assess and improve, we should be looking at the skills of the three individuals in each team, directorate and division, and also look at their skills as a unit.

The team: What do we mean by team? I was taught to think of teams in terms of twenty people, so I tend to use that as a rule of thumb when breaking groups down. If you are going to identify a group of people that manage a team, then twenty people is a manageable group. If you are looking at someone running a team of five, you will probably be too granular. If the lowest level of manager you are working with has 100 people working for them, then you are probably too high level. Of course, this is just a guideline. If you have 100 people all doing the same simple job, then maybe that's okay, but it's still a bit of a stretch. If you manage twenty people, you should be close enough to them to know what they all do, so that normally works for me.

Understand Current State

Once we've set the project up, we need to understand what is happening at the moment. For the example project, I would split this up into four areas:

Where is the problem in the organisation?

To engage the Executive, and to maximise gains early on, we need to know what teams have a problem. An early job is therefore to undertake a desk exercise on the symptoms: In this case, which teams, directorates and divisions have a variance to budget. Specifically, we can consider:

- Variance in spend versus overall budget.
- Variance in activity versus planned activity.

- Variance in spend versus staff budget, broken down as far as we can (e.g. staff group by ward).

We can also look at the level below these symptoms, and consider a whole range of metrics that might help us work out what is going on. These could include:

- Turnover rates by group.
- Employee feedback.
- Staff review rates.
- L&D participation.
- Training backlogs.
- Vacancies.
- Bank and agency use.
- Team diversity.
- Activity per person.
- Sickness absence, both short and long term.

Gathering all of this lot at the most granular level possible, will allow you to understand which teams, directorates and divisions have the biggest issues. It will help you to identify themes that might need addressing at Trust level. And it will help provide a baseline of metrics from which to track improvement. All of this can be done using the standard approach we talked about in redesign: Ask stakeholders what would be useful (with this list as a start), request the data (properly), collect it, analyse it and check it against the challenge.

You should end up with a view that allows you to suggest which teams, directorates and divisions to start with.

What skills need developing and who is already good at what?

Of course, all of that lot can be done by desktop review. The next stage is less likely to be possible through desktop review, because most organisations just don't have an effective view on what skills people have. They have job and role descriptions, but not an objective view on individuals' gaps. Which is a shame, because engagement with individuals in their development is quoted as something that helps retain staff and ensure that they feel valued.

You have two choices here: You can use what the organisation uses, or you can use a bespoke model.If you use the organisation approach, this is a good chance to compare theirs to the standard model and see whether it will meet the requirements. If the organisation model doesn't look comprehensive, then it will need to be enhanced.

Whatever approach you use, you will need to collect a baseline of skills. We need to build a training and development programme that hits the areas that will have the most impact fastest. One of the aspects of that is understanding where the current gaps are in training and development.

Now, you can spend ages assessing the skills that people have, but assessing people's skills is: (a) Time consuming; (b) fraught with difficulties; and (c) can be counterproductive. It is time consuming because you need to assess people, and agree the assessment with them before reporting it. Getting agreement when you have a more negative view of someone's skills than you do is time consuming and is not a lot of fun. It is fraught with difficulties, because you need to be expert in this assessment if you are passing judgement on someone whose career might be affected by your assessment. You'll need to design a process of assessment, evidence and appeal, and do it well. Time consuming again and it is beyond what I believe I am able to do. It can also be counterproductive as you need to be coaching and developing these people, and if you've managed to annoy them by scoring them as a three when they think they should be a five in some spreadsheet somewhere is hardly the best start to your relationship.

So, what is the best way? Self-assessment. We are going to take a coaching approach, so why not start with getting people to assess their own skills. There are a few things to think about when conducting a self-assessment:

Don't just send a spreadsheet out and ask people to fill it in: Get out in a series of workshops and explain what you are doing, and then get people to fill stuff in while you are explaining what each one means and are available to answer questions. Build up a set of FAQs that you can keep updating.

Build a picture on a small set of skills: Using an easy-to-understand scale, not a long list of skills. Nothing kills a self-assessment like getting to question thirty on a SurveyMonkey and just randomly clicking on answers just to get the damn thing over with.

Ask people what they would like to be developed in beyond what is on your skills list: Do this early on with a subset of people (via the steering group) so that these questions can be in the self-assessment from the start, but don't be afraid to add ones right at the end. If they make sense, you can develop them and include them in next year's self-assessment.

I tend to use a scale of 1-5 for each skill: Now, you can use a maturity matrix, where you define the level of skill for each number, but that is horribly time consuming and difficult to read. I have found that you are much better off with a simple scale like:

1 – New to me.

2 – I can do it with help.

3 – I am okay.

4 – I am good at this.

5 – I can teach this confidently.

Useful skills: Skills and competencies that are useful to cover include all of those in the later section.

Ask not only where they think they are, but also where they want to get to: Not everyone will feel that they need to get to teaching level. Not everyone will feel that the skill is useful. They might show "I am at level two on this, and I am happy with that". That's fine, it's all useful information about how they are feeling, and if we do this again next year, you can track not only where they feel they have improved, but also whether their goals have stretched.

Use an interactive mechanism if you can: The main mechanism for self-assessment collection is one in which everyone either fills in a form, or an online survey. That is private and easily tracked. However, if you want something more interactive you can try one of the methods I use for a self-assessment in all sort of setting: The A2 poster session.

Rather than ask everyone to fill in their own form, you can stick large posters on the wall (this works best when you have lots of skills and sub-skills you want to review). You put the posters on the wall and give everyone two stickers for each question: One colour for where they are, and one for where they want to get to. You put a unique number (or their name) on each sticker.

They then stick these up, while everyone else does the same. Or you can sit somewhere central, and staff come through and do this as they walk past. However you do it, you can collect a lot of data on one set of posters, which creates a really useful visual representation of where people think they are and where they want to get to. Of course, this can encourage groupthink, and people might not want to show where they are in front of other people, so this is a just a possible method you can use.

At the end of this process, you should have a matrix that shows you what skills need developing and who needs the most development. In itself you should be able to see:

- Is there a set of skills that lots of people need training in? This would lend itself to a large-scale mass teaching approach.

- Are there teams and individuals that need a lot of training? This would lend itself to personalised individual or team development.

When combined with the view on where the issues are, you can also work out:

- Where are the teams that have the biggest issues, and need developing the most? This is where we may need to put the effort in first.

- Where are the teams that have few issues and are already well developed? We need to note, celebrate and learn from these teams. From experience, I can hazard the guess that it will be down to inspirational and stable leadership in those teams.

What assets exist to help?

If the project team needs to do all the work, then it will be more expensive and less effective than if we can engage the day-to-day mechanisms of the organisation in delivering the change. Delivery is going to require a few things:

Project stuff: We'll need a project manager, someone will need to monitor it, report to the Executive and all that good stuff. This is generally left to the project to sort out, but you might be able to find some helpful project management or PMO resource in the organisation that could help.

Education and training: There is going to be a lot of work around developing and delivering training in the required skills. We deliver a lot of training, and of course a lot of the value comes from experience, but in reality a lot of the content can be found online and in management training guides that are fairly cheaply bought. You will need help in areas such as:

- Course development.

- Digital training development to bring it on-line .

- Training delivery, some of which you may be able to get from the skills that already exist in the teams from the step above.

- Materials development.

- Developing the approach to redesign (unless you use the one in this book).

If the organisation has a training team (it will probably have a few of various flavours), a digital education person, a transformation team, or just people that want to get involved, then lets build on that.

Coaching: Speed of improvement is going to come down to how many good people that you have who can work with managers to help them understand where the opportunities are, undertake redesigns, own their training and development journey and monitor the impacts. As we will discuss, this can be done en-masse, or one-to-one, but there is little doubt that an army of coaches that can work with managers on the front line would create a fast and effective mechanism.

Building a cadre of coaches will really help. These could already exist as liaisons between directorates/teams and central functions, like HR Business Managers or transformation teams. They might be people that are already good at workforce planning and have the most effective teams already. Anyone who is willing to help with this will develop their own skills, so better to use some internal people than all external coaches.

Central change: The solution won't just be about the teams on the ground. Central teams like HR, Finance, Estates and IT will need to assist with the work. These teams need to know what is likely to happen, to understand and engage around the feedback on issues and strengths and help to implement change. Getting representatives engaged from these areas who are freed up to deliver improvements will help speed up rollout.

What specific issues and opportunities are there to improve workforce planning across the Trust?

And finally in the great data collection exercise, comes the listening to people and finding out where we need to improve workforce planning. If you are going out to speak to everyone about their skills, then you can combine the conversations, although you will almost certainly want to extend things out to beyond the managers who are going to be in the cadre for development.

There are a few ways you can go about this:

You can just have conversations with people and record every issue that they raise in a giant spreadsheet: This is a legitimate approach to improvement in any area; just ask people and collate the findings. Later on, you can theme these to create a more compelling narrative than just a list.

You can go out with a set list of issues that you typically find and ask people whether they apply to them: This is another great use of the A2 poster tool approach, one that I have used countless times (alright, round about fifty) when engaging people in cost reduction.

You can combine the two: Ask people about issues, collate them into themes and then go back and ask people the extent to which those issues impact them.

When asking for issues, don't forget to ask for strengths as well. If you just focus on issues, it can be demoralising, and can turn people off. Whenever you present on the issues, you should also point out where there is good practice.

At the end of this approach you will have a, possibly prioritised, set of issues (and strengths), which should also highlight where the opportunities are for improvement. If everyone is complaining about speed of recruitment or the quality of the rostering tool, this may highlight that there is an opportunity to solve that.

And don't forget to analyse and align the data, and to take everything you have learned back to the steering group to engage the stakeholders in what you have found.

Design the Future State

If you remember from the redesign approach, designing the future state mainly starts with bringing together some materials for engagement. And you will have learned a huge amount from the data collection. When redesigning, you would typically take the large stakeholder workshop approach, but when developing this programme, there is a lot more pre-work that can be done.

What you are aiming for here is a picture that answers the following questions

Where is the opportunity based on the data? Depending on the challenge, this will be couched in terms of vacancies, money, missed demand or whatever is important to the organisation. It should set this out for the organisation and through the structure (divisions, directorates etc). We should be clear on what all the effort will bring in terms of impact for the organisation, and people.

What skills need developing and how? What needs a large-scale teaching approach and what needs one-to-one coaching? We should be able to see heat maps of development opportunities across the teams, compared with areas that are doing it right. We will also need to be able to describe:

- How do we aim to deliver training?
- What does the training programme look like?
- What is the approach to coaching?

What do these tell us together? Information on where we have the "perfect storm" where the data says there are issues, where the teams say they are issues and where the management skills need improving. Plus information on where performance is already strong, as people can more often believe they can achieve what is already being achieved, than meeting some external benchmark. All benchmarks are evil anyway...

What is the high-level plan? Overall, what are we going to do, when are we going to do it and what do we think the impact will be? We need to explain what metrics we are going to use, how we will monitor this and how we will steer it. We need to set out a plan for how we will identify organisation-wide programmes to support redesigns, how we share knowledge on redesign progress and how we raise barriers to be addressed by the Executive or Steering Group.

We need to set out this information, and then engage stakeholders in this journey. This will include:

Steering group: As these are the experts, what do they think? They will need to understand the extent of the issue, and help set the expectation on delivery.

Potential helpers: What ideas do people in the organisation have about how they can help with this? This will be based on the asset review, but as the vision comes together, it is possible that more people can be recruited to help.

The development group: We need to share the initial thoughts with the management cadre that are going to be developed to get their views.

Overall, you want engagement in the plan. You typically have more of a straw-person idea going into engagement than you would in redesign, because much more of this is based on the current understanding of data and an expertise in development. However, you would be foolish (and I've done this before, so just take my word for it) to go straight in and implement change without it.

Model the Future State

Modelling in this case is slightly different to redesign, but you will need to work out, from the data that you have collected and the engagement around the future state, what outcomes do you see being delivered, and by when. This will form the basis for the business case (which may be needed to trigger investment for the next stage), for monitoring and for evidencing the benefits of the programme over its life.

Implement

Finally, we get into implementation. Which, as you remember includes not only implementation, but planning for it as well. So we need a good business case, we need a detailed plan and we need benefits realisation in place.

The actual implementation of this has pretty much been covered, but the main areas are:

Project: You'll be running the governance for this across an extended timeframe, possibly six months, probably years. At some point, this needs to become business as usual (remember Kotter? If not, go back and have a look at the earlier sections), but in the early days there will need to be PMO and Project Management activities to plan.

Education: You will need to develop and deliver training courses on the core topics, either internally, or finding external options. This will require all the fun stuff around booking rooms or places, monitoring who has been on them, providing materials etc. Digital versions, on-line skills matrices and an annual/ad-hoc review of skills will need to be developed and put in place.

Coaching: Training is all very well and if you want a nice warm feeling that you are making a difference, then train hundreds of people in workforce planning. Knock yourself out. Maybe about one in a hundred will actually use it, but at least you've got a concrete number you can point to and say "I trained 1000 people, and we had an average feedback score of 8/10, aren't we wonderful". The reality is, most people will give you a good feedback score immediately after a course (especially if you finish early, or are even vaguely nice). There are also a few people that wouldn't give you good feedback even if you personally saved them from a crocodile during the drinks break, but in general most people are nice.

If you are going to make a difference, you need to get in amongst them. Remember the pyramid. Or tetrahedron. We need to develop people by getting them to use their learning in real life, to make a success of it, and to prove to the paymasters that this is worth investing in, so they don't get dragged off onto other things.

I'm not going to teach you coaching as a skill, because there are many better people out there who can teach you. I tend to use the GROW approach I was taught (when I can resist the urge not to just tell people what to do): Set GOALS, examine the current REALITY so you really understand what is getting in the way, OPTIONS for achieving the goal and then establishing the WILL, the things that will make you do it. Coaching is a workforce planning skill in my not so humble opinion.

In this case, coaching comes down to a regular (weekly, monthly, ad-hoc) talk to people about what the current state stage has identified as issues, and about their own issues. It's about establishing what they are going to do about it, and then coming back next time and asking how they have done. You help them examine what worked and what didn't work, help them identify what needs to change and what else they may need development and support on, and then you come back again, and again, and again, until these sessions just become about what they have achieved.

I was always taught, that when you coach people, you should typically not care whether they succeed or fail. Despite being a borderline sociopath occasionally (see previous examples for details), even I find it impossible not to care about someone I am coaching. In this case, things get even more complicated, because I may also need to get results, and if someone isn't playing ball, I may need to highlight that further up the chain. It is worth thinking about what role will you play: Will you separate the coaches from those that monitor progress (and who therefore report on the laggards), or will you ask one person (or will you be the person) that has to do both. Worth thinking about before you finalise the plan.

Redesign projects: It is likely that, in solving the issues of the team, a re-design is going to be needed at some point. This is obviously a core skill of workforce planning, but it is tough in its own right. Teams undertaking redesigns will need support to various degrees.

Infrastructure projects: It is also likely that there will be some infrastructure-type projects. These can be simple ones like "we need to change a recruitment form to include this which will attract more young/old/BAME candidates", to, "we need a new scheduling system". These projects should be monitored centrally through a PMO and reported to the teams on the ground that have identified these needs. Each of these projects will need spinning up, resourcing, monitoring and managing.

And there you have it, an impactful, long-term programme to develop workforce planning skills for front-line teams. Let's get onto the skills you need.

Chapter 5.2

Operational Workforce Planning Skills

There are lots of skills that you need for operational workforce planning. The project we have just outlined will need to pick up all of these, as well as the workforce redesign and workforce plan development skills we have already talked about.

The book is just not the place to provide all of the detail on these skills as each are a specialist area, where there are far better people than me always pushing the learning. I would suggest that you get on the Internet, get some books or look for courses on this stuff from your employer where you can. These are the skills that the project we have just discussed will need to develop their responses to, but you won't just be able to pick up the full curriculum from this book.

However, what we can do is explore these in a little more detail so as to at least give you a starting point.

Leadership

Is this a skill, or is this a talent? Is this even the right word? I'm not sure, but I do know that it is one of my big two differentiator abilities in the world of workforce planning. Workforce planning is about having the right people with the right skills in the right place at the right time. And what I mean about leadership here is the ability and skill to care about the people that you work with, the people you work for (service-users) and the organisation you work in. You need to be able to care about all of them, and balance the needs of all; not slavishly following the whims or even the needs of just one or two.

So, one of the words we need to consider is "Care". There are others, but actually caring about your team will make a massive difference. My go-to book for this is John C Maxwell's "Winning With People", but there are many other books and approaches out there that can help you think a lot more about how you build relationships with your team, your service-users and your organisation (or bosses).

In the case of workforce planning, a lot of this is just about being mindful of relationships, talking to people and getting to know them. If you are interested in, and care about, people, you are going to retain them for longer, help them develop as people, get more out of them, have lower absence rates and have a much nicer time of it in general. People will suggest other good people come and work for you, and they will go the extra mile. This is about understanding what is important to them, listening to them, giving them opportunities to develop and to shine, and saying "thank you". It's so much more than that, but being mindful about your team as individuals is a key part of leadership, and operational workforce planning.

The second word I would use is "Vision". It's a part of Kotter, which is about leading change, but it is as important to leadership. A leader should be able to think ahead about what will affect three things: The team, the service-users and the organisations. They then need to develop a vision for the future that will help navigate those changes to the benefit of everyone and create a compelling picture for the team.

The third is "Success". You can't be sure that what you will do will succeed (believe me on that), but you need to be able to pick yourself up from those things that don't work, look at where you are, and start again until you can't do that any more. If you get to that point then you need to take a break from this somehow for your health and that of the team. When you do succeed, you create a buzz that breeds more success. So, know what success looks like, monitor your progress and share the rewards of that with your team.

Finally, let's talk about "Authenticity" as the fourth. People talk about the work-life balance, but work is part of life, and takes up quite a percentage. For me, it's too big a percentage to be fake. Just being yourself is a key part of leadership; doing what you believe is right, not what you are told to do by your boss, your team, your customers or what you read in a management book. People will know where they stand when they understand you and your motivations – and will trust you more as a result.

Leadership is number one in the list, and I have barely scratched the surface, let alone done it justice. But, as I said at the start, it's a topic where there is already a lot of material from basic through to very advanced, so it's not difficult to build a curriculum. And, taking the view on stakeholders and helpers from the last session, why not get in touch with the NHS Leadership Academy to find out what they can offer, and choose the stuff that will make a difference.

Equality, Diversity and Inclusion

As we've said earlier, Equality, Diversity and Inclusion (EDI) is critical in workforce planning, especially regarding your team and your service-users. As with leadership, this is less about skill and more about taking the time to be mindful that your viewpoint on the world isn't the only viewpoint. One thing I've found is that even though I like to think that I am mindful about equality and diversity, I have biases that I didn't even realise. Training in EDI can be a great boost to your ability to manage the team, specifically:

Bias awareness: There are many on-line resources for self-learning about various biases, that are worthwhile.

Specific Ally or Diversity training: The best training I have had in this area has been given by people sharing their life experiences, to help participants understand the impact of managers and service deliverers on them.

Technical training: Specific training on the Equality Act, as well as around policies for recruitment, leavers interviews, complaint handling etc, to ensure that all groups are treated equally.

Capacity and Demand

Throughout my career in workforce planning, cost control and customer service, this one core skill has been of more use to me than any other. An understanding of capacity and demand, and the link between the two of them allows you to understand how many people you need in order to match what is coming through the door, whether it is minute by minute or year by year. This puts it right at the heart of workforce planning.

Understanding demand

For operational workforce planning, you need to understand what you expect to come through the door: The number of people and the amount of effort that their reason to come through that door requires. In a retailer, a customer might come in and buy a cable off the shelf, another may need convincing to buy the right TV. In health and care, someone's need may vary much more wildly, but in any case, we need different amounts of effort to deal with the same number of people. So the first thing you need to be able to do is estimate what is going to come through the door.

The next thing you need to understand, is how much effort it should take to address the needs of the service-users. That is how much effort it **should** take: If you have spare staff around, you may take more time because you can, and if you are all busy you may take less, but the aim is to understand the total likely need for people so then you can make sure that you have them.

Once you have a view on how many, and how much work will be needed, you can make sure that you have the right amount of people at the right time. We will talk about scheduling and rostering in a moment, but the understanding of capacity and demand goes beyond that. My experience has shown me that most good people are happy when they are not too busy and not too quiet. Of course, what people consider is "busy" varies, but being quiet is boring and being too busy is exhausting.

So, you need to be able to balance this in any time period: Long-term, this is often shown in a workforce model (in Excel or WRaPT, for example). This is a mechanistic process, and is covered under modelling in the redesign. For the most short-term though, this is about being aware of what is coming in and adjusting staffing accordingly.

In some cases, this can be a formalised or even digitised process, in others it is more about getting a feel for demand and the capacity of the team you have available. More formal examples are typically found in areas where there are statutory requirements for numbers of people, often in nursing. In these cases, tools such as Allocate's Safecare can be used to register how many people you have compared to how many patients you have, and it can highlight where wards are under- or over-staffed. This gives local managers their view, as well as allowing organisations to redeploy nurses between teams.

But in the moment, this skill is about being able to spot when capacity and demand are out of balance, and having the wherewithal to do something about it. Whether it is something as simple as saying: "Geoff hasn't come in (again), but actually we're not as busy as we thought, so I don't need to bring anyone else in" or "we're quiet and it doesn't look like we're busy, so I'll send Bandele home early because he covered for Mo last week".

Simple management changes (and ensuring that your supervisors or deputies are empowered to make these changes) will create a better alignment of capacity and demand. It can also get more serious, where sudden increases in demand or losses of capacity (I spent far too much of my life worrying about lottery syndicate wins...) may necessitate more nuclear action around shutting off activity.

Training in this area can focus on real-life examples, and building a playbook of how to deal with variations in demand and supply in all its forms.

Activity and demand

There is a difference between activity and demand in terms of how I define them.

Activity is what presents itself and you deal with. Demand is what is needed. Thus if a hundred people turned up at the door for a social care needs assessment, and we provided that for twenty people, our activity was twenty. Our demand was at least one hundred. I say "at least" because there could have been a thousand people who saw the crowd at the door and left it. There could be another ten thousand who need it, but don't even know what a social care needs assessment is. Yet, maybe all we've recorded is twenty, because that's what we processed.

An understanding of demand is a vital part of understanding capacity and demand because these days it is frankly all about demand.

Right at the start of this journey is Population Health Management (PHM). PHM systems like Sollis provide you with information on what the needs of the population are. If you are looking to improve outcomes, the focus on actual need will more likely get you the bang for the buck. The trouble is that this is going to increase demand and activity in the short (and possibly even long-term) because you are going to find more stuff: Outcomes should improve, life expectancy increase, people will have better quality of life, but activity may well go up. This isn't great news when you have small teams to deal with it all, but as a lot of this activity is now preventative, it does bring in the opportunity for greater involvement for less specialised, often scarce, clinical roles.

In reality, we tend to mainly deal with that element of demand that presents itself (I say mainly, because there are many teams out there that do focus on reaching out to those that don't present, just not enough of them). Someone asks for an appointment, they turn up in an ambulance, a Housing Officer or Police Officer refers them, a routine scan picks something up, etc. When this happens, you diagnose, treat (or not), refer on (or not), monitor (or not) and see them on their way eventually. Sometimes they end up on a case list, or on a waiting list.

This demand can become overwhelming in its own right. As anyone trained in Lean thinking will tell you, delay is a waste: People don't sit there in suspended animation and then move on to the next step. People may worsen (or get better themselves sometimes, but you may then have to wonder why they were on the list) while waiting.

People may want an update, which takes up time. You have to report on them, possibly monitor them. You may have started treatment, that then needs to be re-done because the effective time to pick up the treatment has passed. Finally, the thing about delays is that they become acceptable.

That great manager I mentioned earlier ran an accounting centre where invoices were processed. There were thousands of invoices unprocessed at the end of every week, and yet more were coming in. The number grew, the number shrank, but there were always thousands. When he took over, he put in place initiatives to reduce these down to effectively zero. From then, if it ever went over that effective zero at the end of the week, the team were so disappointed that they covered each others' work, they helped each other, they focused on keeping it at zero. Those that had got the number down felt like heroes. Those that kept it there felt that they had done their job. And on those weeks when there were fewer invoices to process, the supervisors could send people home early, which created goodwill, rather than just diving into the pile of unprocessed invoices.

Another story: I worked with a hospital Trust for a long time, that rarely had big waiting time breaches. This was in recent times, so I won't say they never had them, but they had it under control because the administration and clinical teams did what they could to keep it there. When a new Electronic Patient Record (EPR) was introduced, everyone lost track of where the lists were, and suddenly everyone had breaches. Then, it became impossible to catch up, so lists started growing. People just didn't work to keep it under control anymore.

In health and social care, demand and activity is so great, that it is proving impossible to match staffing to it. And as much as workforce planning is about workforce, it is also about demand. So, there are some things to consider:

What can we do to reduce demand? If capacity and demand are two sides of a scale, only by keeping them in balance can we be undertaking successful workforce planning: Capacity must match activity or demand. We then have two things to play with: One is the workforce, the other is the demand. If we can't get the workforce, or enough of it, then demand is another thing to play with. So, you need to consider what you can do:

- How can we make sure that the demand for our service is right? If we are getting people that should not be in our service, we need to focus on helping people, or upstream services understand what they need to do themselves, before creating activity for us. This requires a monitoring of the issue, redesign efforts, and in extremis it may require turning away inappropriate activity.

- What systems can we use to help us? Mechanisms to highlight unnecessary demand are available, often included in the latest EPR system. These can help to identify those service-users that should have gone elsewhere, and can be used to take action immediately, or highlight the case for redesign.

- What other parties can help us? Unnecessary demand is generally down to a need to do something different upstream, whether with the service-user themselves or with a (probably equally stressed) upstream service. ICSs and ICPs are the nascent groups that, at some point, will have responsibility for all providers working as one system, so engaging people in these groups may be a help.

- On the negative side of things, if workforce planning is failing, and there is legitimate demand coming through the door that you can't match with the right people, what do you need to do to turn that tap off? Because just letting all the people through the door will not answer the problem. You might process them, but you won't meet their needs, and you will burn out your people. Overwhelming legitimate demand creates the need for rationing and restrictions of service, and you need to be willing and ready to consider how to address this. When COVID19 struck health economies around the world, legitimate demand overcame the capacity we had to treat it, and rationing, after trying all the capacity side stuff you could do, was needed.

- You can't live in a position where you are building constant backlogs with no plan to address it. Workforce Planning isn't working, so you have to find some way to balance capacity and demand. The choices are not always palatable, but neither is just letting backlogs grow until something goes wrong with the people on the list.

- Life is complicated, and sometimes it is almost impossible to resolve demand issues. Not just the ethical considerations of effectively rationing healthcare, but also the complex financial arrangements that exist with organisations and with staff. Demand can equal income for the organisation and people, so an understanding of who will gain and who will lose from reducing demand is important if you are going to make change happen.

What can we do to clear our backlogs? If you accept that backlogs, beyond a certain point, are bad, then we need to find a way to deal with them. We need a strategy, otherwise our strategy is to leave things to chance or nature. If you are going to set that strategy, we need to consider:

- This is a project. Getting rid of the backlog is a one-off that should be treated like a project, so feel free to use the WRaPT: Redesign approach for it. You will need to set out a vision, have some sort of governance, understand the issue, engage stakeholders in the solution, model it and implement it.

- What is an acceptable backlog? Earlier I spoke about an "effective zero", but not everything can be done instantly, and so therefore isn't really a delay. In the case of invoices, you can only process them if you have a Goods Received Note, and they may take up to week to arrive, so you might leave it a week before you process an invoice to avoid looking for GRNs that aren't there. In a medical context, maybe people need a couple of weeks on a waiting list. I don't know (but you and your team will) so set the acceptable backlog as your effective zero.

- ***What can we do about demand?*** A review of the current backlog can identify different solutions for different people. Some people will no longer need help, others may need to be seen again, whilst others definitely need something specific. A good clinical review will help set a more refined challenge than just a backlog.

- ***What can we do about supply?*** Then it comes down to putting in place more capacity for the short term, which may well reduce your capacity to meet demand in the first place, leading to more backlogs. That's why this stuff needs modelling…

- ***How do we maintain it?*** Finally, we need to make sure that we are monitoring backlogs, and creating the culture where keeping them under control is rewarded.

Right, all that lot sounds easy doesn't it? Excellent.

Managing to a Budget

This skill is one that can be easily taught, yet has a big impact, but it relies on understanding capacity and demand. It's also a bit different from the others, because it's a mix of skill and a sort of permission. It's where you start telling people what is important, rather than what the rules are, and start to give them the permission to manage, rather than the duty to hit a target. You'll see what I mean.

The reason why this fits under workforce planning, is that cost control may well be the driver for the programme. Staff costs make up 60%+ of total costs in most health and care teams, and a failure to manage these will most likely be the main reason why costs are higher than expected. You get a whole lot more time and trust from people further up the chain when you are managing your budget as well...

Managing to a budget includes a few things:

Understanding the budget: First things first, you need to teach people to understand what their budget is. What are the costs that make up their budget? What do they have control over, and who has control over the rest? What are staff costs and what do the on-costs mean? What makes up any uplift? What costs are fixed, what varies, and on what basis does it vary?

Before someone can manage to a budget, they need to understand it. In some cases, historic overspends are applied to a budget, or their budget is negative, or they are expected to be negative even if their budget is set to a positive number. They may have a CIP target. All of these things need to be explained to people, or how else are they to understand things?

Understanding cost statements: They then need to understand how they monitor it and how they are monitored on their cost control performance. They also need to understand how they can check that everything is accurate and what makes up each line. In short, they need to trust what they are being given and know how to make changes that will help them meet it.

Understand the service-specification and activity: Cost is but one part of the balance when delivering a service. What that service looks like and how many times it is needed makes up the other part. The manager will need to know what is expected for that money (and for the workforce). Including a view on how things vary from that is also useful; often we find that teams are over-delivering.

Agreeing or challenging the budget: People need a chance to be able to agree and challenge budgets. It never ceases to amaze me that people are given budgets that they aren't asked to agree to, yet it's happened to me more than once. It's like someone just wants to hand you a problem. They know you won't be able to stick to it, but fool themselves that by giving someone else responsibility, they are no longer accountable. People need the chance to challenge the budget.

They tend to start with the bits they can't control, complaining about the central 30% charge etc, but once you've convinced people that they need to focus on what they can change, they need time to understand whether it is possible to do what they are being asked to do: Deliver a service to a certain quality with a certain budget.

Finally, they should be asked to agree the budget. If someone doesn't sign up to delivering something, it's a bit tough to hold people to account for it later on. And if the reason they won't sign up to it is because it can't be delivered, then you are only fooling yourself if you don't work together to set something that can be delivered.

Making changes: If budgets are not being met, either historically or because there is a required CIP, then changes need to be made. This can be done through coaching or redesign, but I also use a tool for helping people to identify where the opportunities are. They'll be more about that in the Bumper Book of Healthcare Cost Reduction, available at some point in all good bookstores.

Playing with variable costs: And this is where we come to the big nub of this one, and on to that thing called permission. When you sign up to a budget, you don't sign up to deliver it no matter what happens. Despite your best intentions, all the staff might leave due to that Lottery syndicate payout, or they might all be eaten by wolves or something and you need a sudden doubling of your bank and agency staff (with attendant price).

When stuff happens, you need to be able to deal with it, understand, and record the impact on your budget. The more likely scenario is that activity will change, for example, you agreed something, and now 50% more work is coming through the door. You do what you can (see previously) to control that demand, but if it is happening, you have to deal with it by increasing capacity, which will almost certainly increase costs. At this point, you need to give yourself permission to do it, but again, understand the impact.

So at the quarterly review you can be clear on why the budget should change, and why you need help with the activity in the future.

Coaching and Mentoring

Coaching and mentoring is another specific skill, which we mentioned earlier. Coaching and mentoring are two different but similar things: Coaching is when you help someone to find their own answers to their issues, mentoring is when you help someone to solve their issues with your experience (from which they learn).

The specific skill to teach here is the ability to coach, which managers can use to help develop their team, in order to better meet the needs of service-users. We discussed the GROW model earlier, and it's a worthwhile one to train on. There are many great coaching trainers out there who can provide the course and content, and there's a lot of information available to develop your own learning materials for teams.

Scheduling and Rostering

Blimey, we're getting well into this, and we've barely seen a proper workforce skill at all. That's the trouble with workforce planning, as we may have mentioned (just a few times), it is heavily integrated with everything else that we do. But at long last, we are at some pure workforce skills.

Scheduling or rostering staff is done primarily on a weekly to annual basis, and it's a skill that relies heavily on understanding capacity and demand. It's the skill of planning the matching of your staffing capacity to the activity or demand you are going to face.

Training in scheduling is quite dependent on whether you are supported by a digital package and which one it is. Just remember that training in the package is not actually training in how to roster or schedule. In my experience it has been a common mistake in implementing rostering software to train people in the software without properly implementing the difficult changes needed to do rostering properly.

ANNUAL SCHEDULING

Annual scheduling is about understanding the patterns of demand across the year, and identifying how many people with what skills will likely be needed each week. You play with variables such as how many people you have, taking account of the need to provide annual or parental leave, training weeks and covering annual events like conferences. In a perfect world, of course, you would know everyone's holiday plans to the day right at the start of the planning year, but of course life doesn't work that way. People might have a couple of weeks planned (although these may still change) but the rest might be vague. People don't need to tell you. So the skill is in:

Mindfully undertaking an annual process: So you can identify how many people you need each week, based on an understanding of demand. This might be what you are contracted to do each week, or based on historic patterns, but you need to build a picture (or set of pictures) that show the staffing need.

You then need to gain as much information as you can on the availability of people: If you have a positive relationship with the team, this helps, and sharing the staffing requirement with them is a good way of building on the relationship to get a view on when they are likely to be available. This is a good time to discuss how many people are planning to go to which annual events: I've seen teams all want to go to the same conference, which can play merry hell with your plan...

You also need to get an agreed set of rules in place to govern when time is taken off: There may already be organisational rules (e.g. need to give six weeks' notice of holidays, no more than three weeks off at a time), but even if there are, it is still a very good idea to get agreement from the team that everyone is signed up to them. The rules you are going to need are dependent on your demand pattern, but may include agreeing that at least X of a particular role are always available at all times, and rules to govern how clashes are handled (e.g. first come first served, or based on who chose first last year).

The whole "rules" thing is critical if you are going to match capacity to demand. The more flexible and predictable your team are willing to be, the easier it will be. This will require you to be flexible and predictable as well.

Updates: You will need to adjust as you get closer, so you also need to constantly update the picture. This is again based on communicating with the team.

You can record your annual plan in Excel, with the names as rows and with weeks as the columns, recording who are likely to be available against the activity/ staffing need. If you are looking at annual demand, don't forget to look at the modelling pages in the redesign section of this book for more tips on annual workforce planning.

SHORTER TERM PLANNING

Typically, this is done week by week, although some people work on fortnightly or monthly rotas. Nursing, for example, is often done on fortnightly patterns. Junior Doctor rotas can be far more complex, as can multi-disciplinary theatre teams, and

I am not even going to start getting in to the detail of those specialist rotas.

Yet again, you need to have a view on what demand is likely to be across each week and across each day. This is where software can be a big help, but even without it you can calculate when you are likely to be busiest (number of people multiplied by the amount of work for each one) and work out how many people you are going to need.

Then, again, you need to match people to this level of staffing demand. There are quite a few things to take into account:

Safe staffing levels: You may have to maintain certain staff levels, based on how many people there are, no matter what is actually needed.

Minimum staffing levels: Even if you have nobody coming in for a few hours, you may still need to have at least one person there. You may have to have a minimum of two, just for safety, or to cover a large area. With minimum, and sometimes with safe staffing levels, you need to be aware of downtime and help people use that effectively, to do admin, on-line training etc.

Reasonable shifts: You need to give people reasonable shifts. If you have a peak of demand for an hour, you can't generally expect someone to come in for just that hour and then go home again.

Rules (again): The rules that people set for their working patterns are often the single biggest issue that you will have matching staff to demand. In retail it generally wasn't that difficult as most people were available for pretty broad times, often any time of the week, or with some restrictions around childcare or spouse work times. In health and care we have been so short of staff that we've often had to meet very restrictive staffing patterns.

Sometimes these have been restrictive for legacy reasons (one person I worked to help roster was still working only school hours to look after their kids even though they had left home three years previously), to optimise bank shifts or just because they've been able to choose. Yet again, much of this comes down to setting out the demand patterns to teams, and working with people to optimise the match and reduce the restrictive rules as much as is possible. It's not going to be easy, and may not even be possible, but every bit of flexibility helps the match.

Inefficiency: Waste is a natural part of life, and whilst I keep talking about optimum matches and minimising waste, you have to remember that I am a robot (see earlier). Life is about more than exact matching of people, and the odd busy rush and the odd quiet hour or afternoon is part of life. So don't get too hung up on it. However, it's best to match as well as you can, taking into account legitimate needs of staff, as real life never matches the plan. There are two main wastes to monitor:

- **"Wasted" hours:** The aim of rostering is to minimise the "wasted" hours (the time where we have more people planned to be in work than we need). Small numbers of these hours can be used to target other tasks (admin, on-line training etc) but a good match to demand should be the aim.

- **Lost contracted hours:** If you have a contract to use someone 40 hours a week or 75 hours a fortnight, and you don't use them, you still need to pay them. We call these "lost" or "unused" hours. You really want to avoid these, and if you can't, at least draw attention to the fact so you might get some flexibility later...

Rota checks: If you manage multiple teams, then you should be monitoring the rota performance in advance, in real time and afterwards. Many electronic rostering systems allow for this monitoring. In advance, you should be able to see how complete planned rotas are six, four and two weeks prior to shifts. In real time, you should be able to review final rotas the week before to check how good they are, so as to allow discussion and coaching with team leaders. And after the case, you should be monitoring "wasted" hour levels and variation to planned demand.

Automatic matching: When using an electronic rostering system, you have to let it know the rules that your staff require, and restrictions based on the way you expect staff to work (e.g. no day shift after a night shift). The less restrictive you make this (plus how well your demand behaves) will determine how easy it is for the software to match effectively. Monitoring the automatic matching percentage is a good way of identifying the level of challenge that the manager of each team faces.

As an addendum to this, managers often ignore the automatic matching, and instead spend their (quite often, personal) time writing their own rota, and then adjusting the automatic one to match. This is not good, and should be coached through. Best case, there is a lot of wasted time, and the system is not genuinely helping the manager. This can be resolved. Worst case, the manager is applying their own biases to the rota.

And finally, you always need to remember that workforce planning is a balance between staff and demand. It can be tough to match staffing to unpredictable or spiky demand patterns, so one option is to not even try to do that, and instead change the way in which demand works. It is not always possible, but always remember that you can influence demand or activity. For example, if you have a conference that all your medics are hoping to go to, plan to do fewer operations or clinics that week, and do a few more in the weeks before and after. If you have a dead two hours planned in, can you offer an open clinic to clear up some of the backlog? You will know better than me how much you can influence demand, but always consider it as an option.

Managing Time and Attendance

The final big skill to play in is the managing of time and attendance. You'll need to manage this on a few levels:

Day to day: People need to arrive when needed and stay to the end of their shift, unless demand patterns don't require it. Building flexibility with the team so that short term changes in demand can be matched by the team, will help you be more successful with workforce planning at the operational level.

Sickness/short term absence: People will need to take short term absence for illness, bereavements, etc, beyond the planned parental, annual and training leave. Managing this time requires you to consider whether the actual demand pattern needs you to bring in cover or not. In addition, managing short term absence includes:

- HR systems: A bit like rostering,

much of the training in this area will be based around whatever system the organisation uses to help manage absence.

- Recording and monitoring: A key aspect of managing anything is recording and monitoring this as a team, and as individuals. As well as recording the number and length of episodes, you can also calculate a Bradford Factor for each person. This is calculated as E squared multiplied by D where E is the number of instances and D is the total number of days absent, in a one-year period. As you can see, this approach magnifies the impact of multiple short absences.

- Undertaking back to work interviews. A back to work interview should be held after any absence. These don't have to be heavy and should be short and informal, but they do provide a chance to:

    - Make sure that the person is well enough to return to work and look at support needs.

    - Look at the patterns of absence, and flag if they are nearing or have hit any thresholds for more formal monitoring.

    - Discuss if anything needs to change, or if they need an update on what happened while they weren't around.

  There is a lot of information on the Internet on how to run a back to work interview on-line, so pulling training together on this can be quite easy, and there are specialist providers who can provide a wealth of experience as part of their training.

- Addressing concerns: I'm not a big fan of all the heavy stuff when it comes to absence management, although it has its place when people are misbehaving. In those cases, strict managing to policies is about your only defence. But mostly, absence management is about understanding your team: What triggers the need for absence, and how can you best help the team and individuals to avoid it where possible? Information from back to work interviews is one source, but maintaining communication with the team is another way of understanding issues that the team face which might cause unnecessary absence. Most people will take absence at some point and you should be expecting that.

Long-term sickness: The management of long-term sickness or absence (generally considered to be four weeks plus) again includes the elements of communication and understanding. Sometimes people have short-term absence, that extends into long-term absence, whereas others know straight away that they will be off for some time. Your first jobs are to make sure that the person is supported (sometimes, work is their main or only social support) and to understand what the possible scenarios are. Once you know as much as you can about the situation you can then take other actions, including:

- Communicating this to your bosses in a futile attempt to get budgets adjusted. You can at least try: At least engage HR for advice, and finance to understand the impact this will have on your budget.

- Working out how you need to change your workforce to account for the changes.

- Developing a plan with the person as to how you will monitor, check in and learn about changes.
- Developing a return plan.
- Understanding what needs to change in order to help them return, or ensure that others do not face the need for long term absence.

Basically, your supply of resource has changed, so you need to do some immediate workforce planning to cope in the short term, and some introspection and planning to help the individual and the team in the medium to long term.

Other Skills

There are a host of other skills that you will need as a front-line manager, and that can be trained on. These include:

Policy & process: People need to know all the workforce policies and processes that apply to their teams. This is something that can be easily trained on.

Giving feedback: It amazes me how hard people find this, but learning to constantly provide and seek feedback, how to give feedback and understanding the importance of positive feedback in senior positions is a very useful management skill. If you see workforce planning as the science of ensuring that the team has the right skills, attitude and behaviours.to match demand, then providing feedback is a core mechanism in helping people develop themselves .

Managing conflict/ building a team: My go-to book for this is Patrick Lencioni's, "The Five Dysfunctions Of A Team". We need to start with the simple realisation that one of the key jobs of a manager is building an effective team for the good of the people in it, service-users and the organisation as a whole.

Once we understand that, we ought to focus on making that a reality. There are many ways of doing that: Team building sessions or the use of Myers-Briggs analysis or similar are other mechanisms. But reading, and discussing the Lencioni book provides a nice framework for understanding the dynamics that can get in the way of team performance.

Patient, carer and service-user engagement: If the above is about being mindful of the team, this is about being mindful of the needs of your service-users. It is simply about the skills and attitude required to talk to your service-users and understand what they need. Sometimes it can be the simplest things that make the difference, like a bit of dignity. There are a couple of things to consider:

- One-to-one Engagement: Just talking to people that are using the service while they are in waiting rooms/areas, or are waiting for onward transport about their care: What is bad and what could be improved. What would make life easier and what are the little things that get in the way?
- Engaging experts: In your own organisation you may have teams that engage with service-users through other groups. Finding out who they are and engaging their help in understanding the needs of your service-users, or those that should use the service but don't.
- Formal patient engagement: The use of surveys, focus groups or patient

engagement sessions where staff sit down with service-users and understand their needs. I've used this technique to identify why DNAs were so high, develop a case for one-stop clinics (you won't believe the journeys that some people need to take when they don't have cars. It's like the Odyssey. Only with scarier monsters.)

Permission: I've left this one until last, but it is still important. In lots of organisations I have worked with, the organisation has beaten innovation and risk-taking out of teams. They've been told they can't change a lightbulb, put up a shelf, change a form or let staff leave early. I'm not saying that you can give carte blanche to people to do whatever they like, but I've rarely got into actual trouble for just doing stuff that makes sense.

Helping managers to understand what management is, and to feel empowered to make things happen, without acting in a cavalier fashion is an area littered with danger, but an area that can help you create a much more fun, innovative and flexible culture. Not an easy one to train on, but it is one that can be developed on if you bring the people that are perceived as "blocking" progress and those that are on the front line to talk through a few things. You'll often find that the barriers are in people's minds rather than reality. You'll also be feeding back to those people that are blockers as to what impact they are having, which may lead to improvements.

I am sure that there are many more skills that are useful, but this lot are a good start. Of course, the skills we covered in previous sections are also useful for operational front-line managers as part of annual planning or involvement in system-wide redesign. Just master everything in this book, and then teach your friends and colleagues, because we need an army of people with these skills as we redesign health and care for the future.

Workforce Planning

Conclusion

So, that's it for the Operational Workforce Planning section. We covered the project first, setting out how you can make this sort of work relevant to the executive teams of your organisation or system, so that you can get the time and resources to develop workforce planning skills across your front-line teams.

Then we were onto the skills that you need to have if you are to be able to manage workforce on the front-line. There wasn't a lot of detail, but we have set out the skills and behaviours that you can research further.

And that is also it for the book. I hope you agree that this was truly a Bumper Book of Workforce Planning. We've included a lot here, from what workforce planning is, to why it is so difficult and the vast array of skills that you need if you want to master it.

We've tried to help you develop those skills with approaches to redesign and to planning. We've also listed out a lot of operational workforce planning skills you can learn, as well as everything we know about workforce hubs.

Further reading, and a glossary is included next to help you take the next step in developing your skills in this area. Don't forget, workforce planning is just about the most important job, and the greatest opportunity, that there is in Health & Care management at the moment. Good luck with it.

Further Reading and Resources

Carados Ltd - Provides a YouTube channel with free training videos on everything covered in this book. Search for Carados Workforce Planning.

HEE Star - Health Education England's Star tool includes a directory and a facilitated workshop to help Health & Care systems identify workforce improvement projects and learn from a wealth of available resources.

CLEAR - The Clinically Led workforcE and Activity Redesign is a Health Education England and 33N education programme to develop clinicians in using activity data to effect workforce and system redesign.

SWIM - NHSI/E's System Workforce Improvement Model provides a maturity model for the development of System Workforce, including information on Workforce Infrastructure & Hubs.

Six-Step - Skills for Health's Integrated Workforce Planning approach includes on-line training resources free for healthcare professionals.

Minto - Barbara Minto's book,The Pyramid Principle: Logic in Writing & Thinking, helps you communicate ideas clearly and succinctly.

Kotter - Dr Kotter's book Leading Change sets out an 8 Step Process for Leading Change.

Maxwell - John C Maxwell's book, Winning with People helps people improve relationship skills.

Lencioni - Patrick Lencioni's book, The 5 Dysfunctions of a Team, helps managers deal with conflict within teams

Myers Briggs - Myers Briggs Type Indicator personality tests are a mechanism for understanding roles within teams.

GROW - Sir John Whitmore's book, Coaching for Performance: Growing People, Performance and Purpose, sets out a model for coaching.

Mentimeter - Interactive presentation software.

SurveyMonkey - On-line Survey tool

Glossary

A&E - Accident & Emergency

AHSN - Academic Health Science Network

AI - Artificial Intelligence

ALB - Arms Length Body

CIPs - Cost Improvement Plans

CLEAR - Clinically-Led workforcE and Activity Redesign

DNA - Did Not Attend

EDI - Equality, Diversity & Inclusion

ESR - Electronic Staff Record

FBC - Full Business Case

FTE - Full Time Equivalent

GIRFT - Get It Right First Time

GROW - Goals, Reality, Options/ Objectives, Will

HEE - Health Education England

HiPo - High Potential (individual)

ICP - Integrated Care Partnership

ICS - Integrated Care System

L&D - Learning & Development

LMC - Local Medical Council

NHSI/E - NHS Improvement/ England

NICE - National Institute for Health & Care Excellence

NWID - National Workforce Intelligence Dashboard

OBC - Outline Business Case

ONS - Office of National Statistics

PESTLE - Political, Economic, Social, Technological, Legal, Environmental

PHM - Population Health Management

PID - Project Initiation Document

PMO - Programme Management Office

QOF - Quality and Outcomes

RoI - Return on Investment

RPA - Robotic Process Automation

RTT - Referral to Treatment

SLM - Service Line Management

STP - Sustainability & Transformation Plan or Partnership.

SWIM - System Workforce Improvement Model

ToR - Terms of Reference

WRaPT - Workforce Repository & Planning Tool

For Pam

With thanks to my management mentors over the years, especially Nigel Coates, Dr Sheriff Abdullahi and Stephen Welfare.

And to all those who have directly worked on the WRaPT initiative (especially my co-authors Fiona and Amina), Fran Riley (and her sister), Kirstie Baxter, Jen Hughes, Joanne Smith, Rachel Burnham, Dr John Jeans, Mo Arif, Natasha Lewry, Craig Barratt, Dr Shruti Dholakia and to everyone at Lancashire & South Cumbria NHS Foundation Trust and Health Education England.

This book is dedicated to the hard working staff of the Health & Care professions.

About the Authors

Colin Lewry has been involved in workforce planning since 1994, designing workforce models in a range of industries. Since 2005, this has been done almost exclusively in the health and care sector, with a focus on developing skills in managers and front-line staff. As well as a career in operational and training roles in retail, Colin has been a Director at PwC and Senior Partner at GE Healthcare Partners. Colin currently runs Carados, a health & care management development company.

Since 2013, he has been the Director of the Workforce Repository & Planning Tool (WRaPT) team.

Fiona Lord has worked in the NHS since early 2003, the majority of her career spent in workforce planning and strategy. Starting in a Workforce Development Confederation then joining the Cumbria and Lancashire Strategic Health Authority and later HEE. Throughout this time, Fiona has worked in areas of student data, workforce planning, benchmarking, training development and delivery and managing specific workforce related projects.

Since late 2015, she has led the WRaPT Service developing both the tool, approach and service.

Amina Jina started her NHS career as a Financial Assistant whilst on placement from University. For the last ten years, she has been operating in the workforce planning arena in many Workforce Roles - Analyst, Information Lead, Business Partner and Planning manager. Amina has a Postgraduate Diploma in Strategic Workforce Planning.

She has been working at Lancashire & South Cumbria NHS Foundation Trust with the WRaPT team since 2017.

Fiona Lord, Author

Amina Jina, Author

Colin Lewry, Author

Stephen Welfare, Contributor

WRaPT

WRaPT started back in 2013 as a joint venture between Health Education England (HEE), Lancashire & South Cumbria NHS Foundation Trust (L&SCFT) and GE Healthcare (GE). At the time, both HEE and L&SCFT were keen to develop a tool that allowed front line teams to plan their workforce by mapping their people to activity whilst allowing the then nascent local systems to quickly upload data across multiple organisations.

The result was the WRaPT tool, a web-based workforce modelling tool for recording workforce, activity and how they are related on a team by team, organisation by organisation basis. As well as recording information, the tool allows for the creation of scenarios based on workforce, activity, efficiency and role changes, as well as safe data sharing across teams. This tool remains free to use by anyone in the health and care sector.

It quickly became apparent that workforce planning was not a discipline that was being done very often at front-line team level, and that a workforce modelling tool needed to sit within a wider framework of workforce planning if it is to be used at all. As a result, the WRaPT team have since developed a simple, free-to-use approach to workforce planning and redesign – an approach that forms the basis of much of what is in this book. The team now focus exclusively on building the skills of managers and front-line staff in all aspects of workforce planning and redesign from individual teams, to the development of system workforce collaboratives and hubs.

Many people have been instrumental in sustaining this initiative including: Kirstie Baxter, Fiona Lord, Amina Jina, Fran Riley, Jen Hughes, Joanne Smith, Damian Gallagher, Mike Burgess, Craig Barratt, Dr Shruti Dholakia, Dr John Jeans, Stephen Welfare, Prof. Chris Cutts and Emma Schofield.

For more information, go to www.wrapt.org.uk

Printed in Great Britain
by Amazon

83791028R00106